SEASON OF DEAD WATER

Season of
Dead Water

EDITED BY HELEN FROST

Breitenbush Books, Inc.
1990

First edition. 1 2 3 4 5 6 7 8 9

Library of Congress Cataloging-in-Publication Data

Season of dead water / edited by Helen Frost. — 1st ed.
    ISBN 0-932576-82-6 (cloth) ISBN 0-932576-83-4 (paper)
    1. Prince William Sound Region (Alaska)—Literary
collections. 2. Oil spills—Environmental aspects—
Alaska—Prince William Sound Region—Literary
collections. 3. Wildlife rescue—Alaska—Prince William
Sound Region—Literary collections. 4. American
literature—20th century. I. Frost, Helen.
PS509.P68S44 1990
810.8'0327983—dc20   90-1560
                                            CIP

Breitenbush Books, Inc., P.O. Box 82157, Portland,
Oregon 97282
James Anderson, publisher; Patrick Ames, editor in chief
Design by Ky Krauthamer

Cover art by Sallie Bowen
Dedication page art by S. Rajnus
Cover design by Marilyn Auer

Breitenbush Books are distributed by Taylor Publishing
Co., Dallas, Texas

Manufactured in the United States of America

Contents

*Think of the release
of all those bird and otter spirits.
It is the way it is.
It couldn't be otherwise.*

—Morris Graves

Foreword

Literature is the written expression
of revolt against accepted things.
— Thomas Hardy

One may ask, what is the use of a book like this? These verses and paragraphs, these thoughts, these expressions of outrage and sorrow—who listens and who cares?

In a glossy cover article some weeks ago *US News & World Report* published a reassessment of the Valdez oil spill. According to that report, the environmental damage was not as great as it was first feared to be. Despite some hundreds of miles of soaked beaches and glistening rocks, despite the death toll in land and sea life, the perhaps permanent interruption of community life, repair was underway: Nature and sufficient money would make up the losses in due time.

Setting aside for the moment the accuracy of the report and its probable hidden intent, it is the immediate shock of such a cover story that arouses my misgivings most, being a particularly striking instance of confusing the public mind. For some painful months, by universal agreement, the oil spill is a catastrophe; then, suddenly, it is not. The implications in this revision of events are disturbing: nothing is true except what serves this or that particular interest. In any case, no truth as such.

It is precisely some part of that truth we seek and hope to find in these poems and essays. If I were given a wish in the matter, it would be that the publication of a collection of writings like this would provide us with, not a slight and easily forgotten memorial, but such a clear expression of grief and anger, with so forceful an affirmation of a will to change, that no one, in government, in industry or in private life, would be able to ignore it. I don't expect this to happen, though it does not seem to me an unreasonable desire. In the absence of any such effect we may want to ask ourselves what it is we are doing—whether,

1

in the spirit of the statement by Thomas Hardy, our motives and our talents can justify the attention we often demand for them—those of us who write and publish, and who can on occasion claim to speak for others.

I suppose that, if we were to be coldly realistic about it, we might describe a good deal of the public handwringing and lamentation, the accusations and the multiplying lawsuits, as just another expression of self-interest. It is mainly a matter of money, isn't it—who gets it, and how? Is it really of dire concern to a salmon whether it is suffocated in oil or strangled in a net? These are, after all, among the forms of death, of which there are many. Is there, finally, a limit to how much we can afford to care about the fate of other forms of life? We must live, at a greater or lesser cost to something: land and water, fish and fowl. Not one of us can claim to be uncompromised in some way, and an absolute honesty will be hard to come by.

But let us take Hardy's statement as I think it was intended to be taken. It is useful and, in the present case at least, just. At the same time, let us not congratulate ourselves for seeming to care where others do not, for having written, with competence or with eloquence, for possessing a skill and a means of expression not available to everyone.

The Exxon official quoted by the editor of this anthology was right, of course: events like the Valdez spill *are* the cost of civilization, have been and will continue to be, and he was more honest in saying so than most of us. Whether the cost is worth it is another matter, and perhaps we are beginning to think and to say that it is not.

John Haines
November 1989

2

Introduction

The movement of water through the world's rivers and oceans, glaciers and storms, and the bodies of everything alive, connects us at the deepest level, making a threat to water anywhere a threat to all life.

On March 24, 1989, an ocean tanker owned by the Exxon Corporation ran aground on Bligh Reef in Prince William Sound, just south of Valdez, Alaska. Its single hull was torn open and oil poured into the water much faster than it could be contained or absorbed.

The news was reported to the world largely in terms of numbers: number of gallons of oil spilled, its value in dollars, length of time for response, numbers of birds killed, blood alcohol level of the ship's captain, numbers of otters rescued, hourly wages for cleanup workers, tonnage of oily waste, number of lawsuits, percentage of credit cards returned, increase in suicide (given in percentages), and on and on.

I listened to all the numbers, and stretched my mind around their significance. At the same time, I remained alert for those details which evoked a physical response—tears, or "blood-boiling" rage. The water in our bodies is receptive to knowledge which "dry facts" don't give us.

There was an otter on the news one evening, surrounded by oil, holding her dead baby on her back, staring into the camera for one long moment, then disappearing. Responding to the intelligence in her face, I met it with what love and intelligence I could bring to the matter, through poetry. I knew that other people were doing the same, and I knew that no individual intelligence was adequate to speak of what was happening.

I sent out a Call for Manuscripts, as widely as time and my financial resources permitted (I wanted the response to be as immediate as possible, and I began the project before I found a publisher). It read "In the days following the oil spill in Valdez, an Exxon official remarked 'That's the cost of civilization.' The truth and the magnitude of this glib statement has stayed with

3

me, and I have given much thought to such questions as 'What is the cost?' 'Who is paying it for us?' 'How can we hear the voices of the birds, plants and animals, and our own conscience, and each other, over the sound of Exxon's P.R. machine?'"

Responses started coming in—poems, essays, a drawing of a loon, and lots of letters, saying "I'm sorry, I don't dare think about this yet." Or, "I can't." Or, "I don't think I should write about this." Or, "This is about a different oil spill." Or, "This doesn't mention the oil spill, but maybe you will see a relationship." Wendell Berry posed a question of his own: "How did civilization make it for so long without petroleum, much less an oil spill?"

The book has gathered in layers around the hard questions we have tried to face, and it is built on the labor of many more people than those who are named within its pages. In thinking of these layers, I have often said it has "snowballed" but the expression "pearl of wisdom" also comes to mind, perhaps more closely describing this process of seeking some small but enduring truth.

From Walter Meganack, Sr., Chief of the village of Port Graham, I have taken the title, *Season of Dead Water*. The small optimism it implies is all we are entitled to. We have no idea how long or how barren the season will be, or who will be here to see what follows it, but by naming it a season, we look beyond it.

The oil cannot be cleaned up—the most anyone hopes for is dispersal, and that dispersal brings it eventually into all of our bodies, which is to say into our emotions, our intelligence. I believe that it is there, if anywhere, that some sort of purification can happen. The contributors to this volume have begun, and in your thoughtful reading you also contribute to, this healing work.

Helen Frost

WILLIAM STAFFORD

Roll Call

Red Wolf came, and Passenger Pigeon,
the Dodo Bird, all the gone or endangered
came and crowded around in a circle,
the Bison, the Irish Elk, waited
silent, the Great White Bear, fluid and strong,
sliding from the sea, streaming and creeping
in the gathering darkness, nose down,
bowing to earth its tapered head,
where the Black-footed Ferret, paws folded,
stood in the center surveying the multitude
and spoke for us all: "Dearly beloved," it said.

WALTER MEGANACK, SR.

When the Water Died

This is an edited version of remarks Walter Meganack, Sr., the Port Graham village Chief, prepared for a conference of mayors who met June 27, 1989, in Valdez to review the oil spill's impact. The speech was read by the village council secretary, Elenore McMullen.

The Native story is different from the white man's story of oil devastation. It is different because our lives are different, what we value is different; how we see the water and the land, the plants and the animals, is different. What white men do for sport and recreation, we do for life: for the life of our bodies, for the life of our spirits, and for the life of our ancient culture.

Our lives are rooted in the seasons of God's creation. Since time immemorial, the lives of the Native peoples harmonize with the rhythm and the cycles of nature. We are a part of nature. We don't need a calendar or a clock to tell us what time it is.

When the days get longer, we get ready. Boots and boats and nets and gear are prepared for the fishing time. The winter beaches are not lonely anymore, because our children and our grown-ups visit the beaches in the springtime and they gather the abundance of the sea: the shellfish, the snails, the chitons. When the first salmon is caught, our whole villages are excited. It is an annual ritual of mouth watering and delight.

When our bellies are filled with the fresh new life, then we put up the food for the winter. We dry and smoke and can. Hundreds of fish to feed a family.

Much has happened to our people in recent centuries. We have toilets now, and schools. We have clocks and calendars in our homes. Some of us go to an office in the morning. The children go to school in the morning. But sometimes the office is empty and locked. Sometimes the child is absent from school.

6

Because there are more important things to do. Like walking the beaches. Collecting the chitons. Watching for the fish.

The land and the water are our sources of life. The water is sacred. The water is like a baptismal font, and its abundance is the Holy Communion of our lives. Of all the things that we have lost since non-Natives came to our land, we have never lost our connection with the water. The water is our source of life. So long as the water is alive, the Chugach Natives are alive.

It was early in the springtime. No fish yet. No snails yet. But the signs were with us. The green was starting. Some birds were flying and singing. The excitement of the season had just begun. And then we heard the news. Oil in the water. Lots of oil. Killing lots of water. It is too shocking to understand. Never in the millennium of our tradition have we thought it possible for the water to die. But it is true.

We walk our beaches. But the snails and the barnacles and the chitons are falling off the rocks. Dead. Dead water. We caught our first fish, the annual first fish, the traditional delight of all— but it got sent to the state to be tested for oil. No first fish this year. We walk our beaches. But instead of gathering life, we gather death. Dead birds. Dead otters. Dead seaweed.

Before we have a chance to hold each other and share our tears, our sorrow, our loss, we suffer yet another devastation . . . we are invaded by the oil company. Offering jobs. High pay. Lots of money. We are in shock. We need to clean the oil, get it out of our water, bring death back to life. We are intoxicated with desperation. We don't have a choice but to take what is offered. So we take the jobs, we take the orders, we take the disruption.

We start fighting. We lose trust for each other. We lose control of our daily life. Everybody is pushing everyone. We Native people aren't used to being bossed around. We don't like it. But now our own people are pointing fingers at us. Everyone wants to be boss; we are not working like a team. We lose control of our village.

Our people get sick. Elders and children in the village. Everybody is touchy. Everybody is ready to jump you and blame

7

you. People are angry. And afraid. Afraid, and confused. Our elders feel helpless. They cannot work on cleanup, they cannot do all the activities of gathering food and preparing for winter. And most of all, they cannot teach the young ones the Native way. How will the children learn the values and the ways if the water is dead?

The oil companies lied about preventing a spill. Now they lie about the cleanup. Our people know what happens on the beaches. Spend all day cleaning one huge rock, and the tide comes in and covers it with oil again. Spend a week wiping and spraying the surface, but pick up a rock and there's four inches of oil underneath. Our people know the water and the beaches. But they get told what to do by ignorant people who should be asking, not telling.

We fight a rich and powerful giant, the oil industry, while at the same time we take orders and a paycheck from it. We are torn in half.

Will it end? After five years, maybe we will see some spring-time water life again. But will the water and the beaches see us? What will happen to our lives in the next five years? What will happen this fall, when the cleanup stops and the money stops? We have lived through much devastation. Our villages were almost destroyed by chicken pox and tuberculosis. We fight the battles of alcohol and drugs and abuse. And we survive.

But what we see now is death. Death—not of each other, but of the source of life, the water. We will need much help, much listening in order to live through the long barren season of dead water, a longer winter than before.

I am an elder. I am chief. I will not lose hope. And I will help my people. We have never lived through this kind of death. But we have lived through lots of other kinds of death. We will learn from the past, we will learn from each other, and we will live. The water is dead. But we are alive. And where there is life, there is hope.

Thank you for listening to the Native story. God bless you.

INGRID WENDT

One of Those Things

Caught up in that extravagant trust of the young, again
today I asked my students: Those questions
you asked when you were little, remember?
If God made everything, who made God?
How does the stork get into the hospital room?
Has it the strength to carry the baby?

It's easy, with them, this playing with wonder,
keeping alive what knowledge would have us deny.
Together we rescue the obvious, each child
my own daughter, my son, writing
Why don't fish drown? or Where does the black
of the night sky begin? Myself

still unable to grasp how the sky just keeps on going
or how the reliable sea could just last week become
other: oil spreading from just one tanker farther
than any human vision: birds, fish, otters
washing ashore in numbers like stars
all of us long ago stopped trying to count.

Today not asking where but when
it will end: that infinite sea
with all its unknowns
once within the grasp of what we still
could imagine, grounding us.
One of those things we knew was forever, for sure.

CHRISTIANNE BALK

Before the Spill: Celebrating the
Sea at Dusk

(Kenai Peninsula, March 23, 1989)

The sky's burnt orange and the sea's burnt orange
streaked with pewter, God, even our faces
glow orange enough right now to make us
talk about another child. Can I hold
this one's hand long enough to keep her dry?
Look, she's filled her mouth with beach gravel.
That's right, spit them out in Mommy's hand, every one.
Watch out! The sea takes anything it wants—
stones arced from small hands, needled starfish,
limpets, loaded tankers, the blue and white rush
of breaking ice, northbound flecks of teal, the seiner
you spent all winter scraping and sanding. This sea
wants everything—the black cod's eye, phalarope,
green fucus, milky clouds of milt, the otter's coat,
the shadowed cracks between each rock along this jagged
coast, sooty shearwater and steel hulled ship,
sea lions thick with pups, razor clams, pot shrimp,
krill, snow crab, barnacles, whelks, plankton drifting
into bloom, halibut, cohoe, chum, the small gray tail
slipping from the belly slit, screaming cliffs
of kittiwakes, tidemarshes filled with snipe,
cranes, grebes, scaup, duck, forty-pound swans,
even the eagle sitting in the dead spruce, waiting
for the red and silver rivers to flow upstream.

W. S. MERWIN

One Story

Always somewhere in the story
which up until now we thought
was ours whoever it was
that we were being then
had to wander out into
the green towering forest
reaching to the end of
the world and beyond older
than anything whoever
we were being could remember
and find there that it was
no different from the story

anywhere in the forest
and never be able to tell
as long as the story was there
whether the fiery voices
now far ahead now under
foot the eyes staring from
their instant that held the story
as one breath the shadows
offering their spread flowers
and the chill that leapt from its own
turn through the hair of the nape
like a light through a forest

knew the untold story
all along and were waiting
at the right place as the moment
arrived for whoever it was
to be led at last by the wiles

of ignorance through the forest
and come before them face
to face for the first time
recognizing them with
no names and again surviving
seizing something alive
to take home out of the story

but what came out of the forest
was all part of the story
whatever died on the way
or was named but no longer
recognizable even
what vanished out of the story
finally day after day
was becoming the story
so that when there is no more
story that will be our
story when there is no
forest that will be our forest

CAROLYN KIZER

Suppressing the Evidence

Alaska oil spill, I edit you out.
You are too terrible to think about.
I X, I double-X you out.
The repeated floods in Bangladesh:
The starving poor that stare at us,
Stare with plaintive smiles,
Smiles without hope
As they clutch a bulbous-bellied child,
I erase your dark faces.
I edit you out.

From the dark windows of their limousines
The rich long since have waved their ringed hands,
Said Abracadabra, to disappear the poor.
Their streets are swept clear
So the homeless are sucked down the dirty drains.
Only their reflections in the tinted glass
Stare back in their complacent discontent:
The blind rich, in their blind car.

On Madison a young emaciated man
In a threadbare jacket, shivers in the snow.
Help me. Please. I have no place to go.
I hold out a dollar bill between his face and mine
Like the fan of an old Japanese courtesan,
Then hurry past as his face turns to smoke.

I flee the city, back to my comfortable farm
In the valley of wine. I drink the wine.
I do not turn on the news.

13

I and the wine will blot it out.
As we erase more and more of the world's terrible map
How may we bear witness, as we should?

I must hold in my mind one small dead otter pup.

CHARLES KONIGSBERG

The Social Function of Catastrophe

We have been reversing the evolutionary process that made our world safe for life . . .

We can now understand that—given our nature as the human species—catastrophe serves the function of reawakening us to the fundamentals of our existence, and of placing all else in that crucial perspective.

The catastrophic nature and magnitude of the Prince William Sound oil spill thus serves to reveal the shallowness and superficiality of so much in our daily lives—our preoccupation with and enslavement to means, to the neglect of ends—while at the same time exposing the pattern of myths which underlies that cultural malaise and its destructive consequences.

Perhaps the most dominant component of that mythic pattern has been the notion that the "economic" (how we "make our living") factor is the most essential element in our lives. This notion assumes, above all, that the economic factor can be understood as separate from all other important elements of our lives. Clearly, this is not so.

Is the Exxon/Alyeska oil spill (with its antecedents and its consequences) but an "economic" matter? Or is it really "political"? Or "scientific/technological"? Or "psychological"? Or "environmental"? "Cultural"? It's all of these, and more.

Each and all are strands of that whole we call "life on earth." That we have given these parts different "names" does not mean that they are separable from the functioning of the whole.

In this perspective, it's clear that we can no longer tolerate the myth that the economics of how we make our living can somehow be separated from the health and integrity of the natural world. It's equally clear, therefore, that neither Exxon/Alyeska, nor the oil industry collectively, have any right to the power they have so arrogantly assumed and exercised over our

15

lives under the mythic cloak of economic separability and priority.

We can now see what a profound and deliberate misconception it has all been.

In this light, two related myths of that supposed self-contained economic world have also been exposed for all to see: the notion that private/corporate business activity is inherently "more efficient" than that of public agencies, and that the private/corporate executives involved are necessarily "socially responsible citizens."

Exxon/Alyeska have laid those myths to rest for all time. Not only did they fail in their planning and readiness for such an "incident," but they also had—in the usual way of those who exercise illegitimate power—carefully concealed their failure and pulled the strings of their governmental allies to deny funding and personnel to our public protection agencies.

It seems clear enough that the failure and its concealment were consciously pre-calculated. They occurred because of the distortion of perspective from the "bottom line"—leading to the financial decision to accept any costs of potential "errors," human or otherwise, which could then be carried, like any cost, as just another "cost of doing business."

To be sure, our public agents also had their responsibilities. These personnel cannot perform as required, however, if the necessary resources are not funded and if the (manipulated) "climate of opinion" discourages enforcement—and if, in the ultimate sense, the people continue to be blinded and misled by the P.R. hype incessantly disgorged by the industry and its camp followers.

The crucial consideration in understanding this issue of responsibility is that responsibility (and accountability) must lie always with those who have and use the power that eventuates in the catastrophe.

We can now see that the operative power in our society often rests not with our public institutions and public authority but with private and corporate holders of power whose influence is concealed from view and protected by continuously repeated myth. Because they believed their power to be hidden, Exxon/ Alyeska played recklessly with Prince William Sound—not only with the Sound itself but with us, our lives and our world. Their behavior has been irresponsible in the worst sense.

Recognition of the pattern of thought and behavior of Exxon/ Alyeska leads to the consideration of yet another basic myth exposed by the tragedy, a myth which forms the framework that underpins the success of the others. And that is the myth that "numbers-dollars-things" are the language of life. We have allowed that myth to dominate virtually every hour of our waking life and, for many, even the life of dream-fantasy.

Once articulated, and we become aware, the gross absurdity of this myth is apparent, which is why those persons and groups whose interests such language serves have ever been quick to turn every issue of public policy and socio-ecological concern into a discussion of numbers-dollars-things: to forestall awareness.

But numbers-dollars-things is not the language of life. It is the language of power. It's not surprising, therefore, to observe that Exxon/Alyeska—having allowed time for our most deeply felt reactions to the oil spill to subside—are pursuing a P.R. campaign to recapture the terms of discussion of the catastrophe: numbers of people, length of booms, miles of coast, numbers and size of boats, and the like, all instantly translatable into impressive numbers of dollars. Numbers, dollars, things—and "Hey, enough emotionalism already!"

What is most important to understand in all this is that whoever controls the terms of discourse or discussion of any public issue also controls the outcome. Numbers-dollars-things automatically and instantaneously diverts attention and concern from the cultural and ecological, life-threatening dimension of this tragic catastrophe, while also fostering dissension and conflict.

It's "Divide and Conquer!"—the industry's expertly practiced tactic of turning any situation to the advantage of its concentrated power.

The basic power over others lies, however, in reconstituting that attitude of mind in which numbers-dollars-things are the unquestioned perspective in which to view all concerns. Once accomplished—if they are permitted to do so—the industry will have re-established its power.

They do indeed know what they must plan for and do. We may contrast Exxon/Alyeska's practiced P.R. with their failure at spill response. "Damage control" was sought, not in containment of the crude.

Once we understand the manner and extent to which myth and language can give illegitimate power to those who wish to control others, we can then begin to take back that power, our power, and make it visible through public authority—public authority which, as the oil spill catastrophe demands, must rededicate itself to democratic principles, among which, it is now clear, the maintenance of cultural and ecological integrity must be given a position of the first rank.

That is the most valuable lesson we can learn from Prince William Sound's tragedy and our own suffering. If we do not, or if we fail to act accordingly, then we are surely the least deserving of species.

PETER DAVISON

Ye Have Your Closes

As grey damp covers this supine July
the mourning dove reiterates her moaning
through endless post-coital afternoons.
These days more lungs take ordinary air,
drain out its oxygen, and mingle it with carbon
than ever. Humans are breathing harder
than ever before in breathless history.

We have taught our children too much about comfort:
warm air, cool drink, hot sound, high speed, ripping
the planet inside out, clawing for carbon
to feed the ravening engines of convenience,
charming fossils out of the ground
to relinquish gases life inhaled from air,
cashing in the earth's bank balance of death.

We have taught our children too much about profit:
they have taken to burning bodies still alive,
forests that have furred the world's broad flank.
If dark and thickness close upon our lungs
and force us back to living under thatch,
on poles, in mists, by fever-blistered seas,
we'll mourn like doves, repeating as we grieve
how carbon kept us whole—and though the whole
world turn to coal, then chiefly live.

RUTH WHITMAN

Cruelty

This human wind spoils everything
it grazes over, leaving spittle on the floor,

on table tops, pages of books. Rolls
salty hot fog across the bay into

this room. Keeps forcing its damp breath
into my ear, an insistent junta of a wind.

It brings poison from Chernobyl, blight
from our tattered ozone. It insults

the wounded ocean, already scarred with oil,
mimicking its primal essence. It is

without mercy, like the boy carrying
his mother's heart to the sorcerer—

heedless, inexorable—who doesn't hear the heart
cry "Watch out!" as he stumbles through the woods.

DENITA BENYSHEK

Journey into the Dead Zone

During April 1989, I travelled to Prince William Sound with Corwin Fergus, an independent filmmaker and photographer. The purpose of our trip was to document the oil spill. During our journey into the Dead Zone, I interviewed folks and kept a journal. What follows are excerpts from these records.

April 16, 1989—Journal: Cordova

Most people I've interviewed thus far are afraid to make strong statements and Exxon has a gag order (against speaking to the press) on the boats it's contracting. Or they make impassioned statements in conversation and when I ask if they'd allow me to record: No way. The eyes are averted. The shades of big brother sunglasses slide on. Silence.

April 18 and 19, 1989—Journal: in Herring Bay, Prince William Sound, with Bird Rescue

Yesterday, and again today, we watch an otter pup, small and motherless, swimming in panic around the edge of the bay. Rising to gulp air then immediately diving, to escape the oil. Not swimming normally along the surface. Tom labels the pup's behavior "porpoising," due to a loss of buoyancy. It is "The Death Dance." "Yeh, that's what they do right before they die." Yet he is still frisky enough to evade capture.

One of the fishermen, a heavily bearded vet and stand-up comedian, is raging about. This morning he'd wiped his nose and gotten oil on it. Now that area is a raw sore.

I overhear the skipper of the *Neva*, "It says here on this piece of paper, you're supposed to hold them by the wings, but I can't find any wings."

April 16, 1989—Interview with Linden Colour O'Toole, Co-Coordinator at the Spill Response Office in Cordova

My family was redoing the plumbing in our house and our bathtub has sat in our front yard now for three weeks, and we've had no hot water. And my children have been farmed out to daycare because I volunteered to help down here at City Hall and subsequently it worked into a full-time position.

It's been very much like someone dealing with a death or notice of terminal illness, with definite stages. At first everyone was in a state of shock. We all began to run and live on adrenaline and fear and stress and a do-what-you-can type of energy. This went on for about two weeks. During this time, many people including myself didn't do their dishes, didn't eat well, didn't spend time with their families. We didn't sleep well. It was totally absorbing. After two weeks, we just began to collapse, physically and emotionally. For several days there, people would just break down and cry. I'd see four or five people a day crying in public.

We are onto a new stage now, of recovery and trying to envision how we can rebuild our lives and hold a positive vision of what life will be. But there is still a lot of sadness, particularly when we think about the wildlife. Someone comes in from working on the spill and they cry for half an hour because it has been so devastating to see sea otters scratching their own eyes out because of the oil. Or a bird pecking a hole in its own chest to try and clean the oil off its body. Or another friend said he pulled up to a buoy with sea lions on it, these beautiful, giant, majestic beasts. They were covered in oil and their eyes were white and decaying right out of their heads. The largest, frightened by the Zodiac, fell off the buoy, sunk, and never came up.

We've been very frustrated trying to get a bird cleaning station here and expand animal rescue efforts; but Exxon is trying to save its money.

At one point, someone brought some of the oiled birds into town and put them, in a cardboard box, in front of the Fishermen's Union. My little three-year-old son saw those and I'm sure he'll see them until the day he dies because he's brought them up maybe ten or fifteen times and that was two weeks ago. I've never heard him do that before. But he says things to me like "Mom, I want to go back and 'safe' the birds . . . I know how we can make them fly, we'll just throw them and they'll fly . . . I want to buy some bird food and feed those birds."

. . . We've had a lot of dissension amongst ourselves because a handful of people were hired by Exxon. Because they paid so much money, some are making $3,000 to $5,000 a day for chartering their boats. And many people, over two hundred boats, have not had an opportunity to make a penny out of this to offset their losses in fishing. The whole economy is based on fishing. It's the laundromat owner, the babysitter, the net mender, the cannery worker.

Here, we live seasonally. We go six to nine months of the year without any paycheck. We do not live in abundance. My husband has been a deckhand for seven years, gradually working his way up to buying a permit. Our most valuable possession is a Martin guitar. In the winter, we live in a log cabin at Sheep Mountain, in the interior, and pay twenty-five dollars per month rent. There are trade offs of affluence and culture. We get a lot of rain and live in a harsh climate; but, we live in one of the most beautiful places on the planet.

Exxon has billions of dollars and can afford to hire fancy P.R. people and is getting a message out to the American people that they've done a great job, they're treating everyone fairly, and they're cleaning up the Sound and doing the best they can. And that's not the case. There are documentable decisions they've made to mitigate the economic impact on Exxon. People would call with equipment or materials to donate. Exxon would never return their calls. Experts called wanting to come and help. There's a list of seven hundred volunteers wanting to help. And they are not used.

I've heard people say that Exxon decided early on it would be cheaper to pay claims than to clean up the Sound.

I've heard through the grapevine that it is difficult for hired boats to talk to reporters because it is written in their contract that they may not talk to the press. A woman said today that she felt she couldn't speak her mind about Exxon because her husband was being paid so highly by them.

April 17, 1989—Interview with Kelly Weaverling, Director of Bird Rescue in Cordova

I don't have an official title, I refer to myself as Commodore just to add a little levity to the situation.

The oil spill occurred the 24th. Everyone in town instantly coalesced. I tried to find out who was in charge of animal rehabilitation and rescue. They contacted me on the 29th to see if I could figure out a way to collect the dead and wounded to deliver to Valdez. Initially, when they inspected the vessels to see how suitable they would be for birds, they were concerned that they needed a warmer, enclosed space. We looked around the (Valdez) harbor, and I said, "What you need is one like that halibut charter." It turned out he'd already been hired by Exxon for bird rescue. I had a look at his log and for three days it said: "Stand by for Exxon bird rescue."

That night we caught our first bird, a common murre.

. . . I arrived here in 1976 from years of wandering mostly in Europe and North Africa. I got a job with a kayak guide service in Prince William Sound. We later became partners. Basically I operated a kayak guide service in Prince William Sound from 1976 to 1980, in the Sound most of the summer. My wife and I then realized that we didn't care for guiding. We decided we'd just come out when the snow left the beach and stay all summer long until the weather got miserable in August. So I sold all my shares in the business. We'd buy four months worth of food, hire a charter boat to haul it, cache it safe from animals and birds. We never stayed in a cabin, we camped and kayaked from place to place from the first of May until the end of August, from 1980 'til 1987. We've skied on the Sargeant Ice Field. We had the first authenticated sighting of the Caspian tern. The Forest Service archeologist gave me a crash course in prehistory and wherever

24

I went, I found archeological evidence. Fish and Game and the Forest Service were interested in locating eagle nesting trees. One summer, my wife and I tagged fifty or so eagle nesting trees. We've engaged in independent ornithological research, attempting to determine nesting habits of the marbled murrelet.

It's paradise.

When I initially flew into Prince William Sound, landed in a float plane just off shore a little spit of land, there was a glacier that came to the sea, calving icebergs. There were mountains with snow all around me. Floating icebergs in the lagoon had seals and otters on them. A pod of orcas blew just in front of me. One of them had a very distinctive bent fin and I've seen him every year since 1976. I realized this was home. There was no reason for me to go anywhere else, ever again.

I don't think the impact on the wildlife can be adequately described. I don't think that video or even overflights can explain just how bad it is out there. All the fishermen in those forty-odd vessels out there, perhaps 150 people, break down into tears at least once a day.

There are dead birds floating in the water. There are oiled loons making their calls, oiled otters and babies. There's dead deer floating in the water. There are animals eating toxic kelp, their normal browse during the winter. There are smaller animals dying in holes. There are birds dying under bushes. There are bear and deer dying in the forest. Barnacles are dead. Chitons are dead. Limpets are dead. It's a dead zone out there. I've described it before as a concept of Hell—and that's close. It's kind of like the desecration of a church or a cathedral. It's just horrible. It's just horrible. I don't know how I can explain it to you.

I'm very afraid for the upcoming migration. Twenty million birds pass through this area between the middle of April and the middle of May. There are times when a hundred and eighty thousand shore birds per hour go by. Canada geese, sand hill cranes, swans . . . As the flyway comes up from the lower forty-eight, it goes from the coast to the Rocky Mountains and is rather broad. The further north you go, the flyway with huge flocks of migrating birds is compressed. The first opportunity they have for feed is in the Copper River Delta (for a very small amount of the birds) and Prince William Sound. It has the potential to be, perhaps, the largest single avian disaster in the history of the world.

According to the author of *Birds of the North Coast, Prince William Sound Area,* the premier bird expert for this area, his estimate is that fifty to a hundred thousand birds died as a result of the initial oil spill. And his best projection is that the migrant birds who come to breed in this area (not the ones that pass through) will be oiled in the tens of thousands. I'm very, very worried.

I bear a lot of responsibility, as I'm sure many people here feel, for not being sure that Exxon had a plan to deal with this thing. Not demanding inspection of the plan. Not demanding to see the equipment and personnel. Not demanding to see test runs done. I moved here to Cordova to retire, to get away from the hubbub and hurly-burly. There's no road to this place and it's a small community. Everyone knows everyone by their first name. My home didn't come with a set of keys because the former owner didn't have any. We don't lock our car doors in Cordova, but even leave the keys in the ignition in case someone needs to move it. Generally we accept people's word and their handshake.

But times have changed now and people in Cordova have become extremely xenophobic. They have no trust. Kind of a sad thing to see; but, as far as retiring to the sleepy little village of Cordova, hiding out in an ivory tower, this oil spill has proven that can't be the case. I'll probably devote the rest of my life to this sort of activity, to make it as difficult as possible for this to occur again.

. . . When the pipeline was first proposed, there was a question as to whether it should go to a marine terminal or be piped overland through Canada. Everyone in Cordova supported the overland route because of a fear of oil spills. With a land route, you can contain the oil where it spills. At sea, you're pretty much out of luck even with sheltered waters on sunny days. I do not support the transport of oil over the ocean. If it can happen, it will happen. If you don't want it to happen, it has to be impossible.

This is not as emotional a story as I've told before. I'm getting a little bit jaded. I still can't eat a meal. I just nibble through the day. At first it was 6:00 a.m. 'til after midnight, and not sleeping well. But it's not a sprint we're running now, it's a long distance race.

April 19, 1989—Interview with Tom Dragt, Bird Rescue Worker

The condition of the shore varies, but the worst I've seen is three inches thick of greasy sludge like thick chocolate pudding. (Our) object is to document all the animal loss incurred by this oil spill. The first few days we were out here, we were rescuing live otters who were oiled up and could barely swim, and birds, and picking dead ones up out of the oil slicks and off the beaches. Mostly now we're finding otters and birds that have already died and the scavengers are eating them. With the otters, it's a kind of sad thing, they've been cleaning themselves, licking themselves. They ingest so much oil that it poisons their systems. And we find them on clean rocks with clean bodies but they're dead because they ate all the oil.

Lots of cormorants. All the sea birds. Murrelets, and murres, and grebes, and scoters and scaups. Lots of loons too. We just run the skiff up to them, we have a long scoop net. We wrap the bird up in oil absorbent cloth and put it in a box. It's transferred to an airplane and taken to the rescue center.

But we were told not to catch any more live otters and it has upset a lot of people. The first few days we were out here, there weren't enough people to catch all the oiled otters. They sent marshals out and threatened to arrest and prosecute us if we caught live otters . . . And we were going ahead and doing it anyway; because, what am I going to do?

That was the last otter I caught live, here in this bay. He was swimming around and he was so concerned with staying afloat and cleaning himself, he didn't even see the skiff pull up. We put him in the boat and he just laid there. I mean, some of the otters that weren't heavily oiled were screaming and biting and nasty upset animals. But this one really got to me. He just laid in the boat and I petted him like a tame pet. I rubbed him down with oil rags and he just moaned. I got really choked up. He didn't stand a chance against the oil.

Then we couldn't find anybody to take him. The guy on the airplane said he wasn't authorized to take live otters, and he didn't want to get in trouble with the Feds. I was absolutely livid. Finally we found some biologists and we gave the otter to them. Then it took another six hours to find a helicopter to get the animal out. I don't even know if he made it.

. . . Exxon has charge of a lot of the helicopters and air traffic, they were shuttling most of the press to the Sawmill Hatchery for the press to see the rescue effort there. Most of the press wasn't out here to see the oil on the beaches, the dead animals, the gruesome things. Rather than seeing people cleaning rocks on the beach: that's ludicrous.

. . . We tend to lead a sheltered life up here because we're out in the wilderness. The power of large corporations has hit home. It's time we started watching what they're doing closer.

PETER SEARS

Oil Spill

The ocean is leather in slow motion.
Waves don't break, they squat and slide.
Stick a finger in—thick as fudge
up and down the beach;

and the fixed, brown bubbles
mean death by suffocation.
May the men who did this
boil and roll in a sea coat of oil;

and may their superiors
join us and our neighbors
on our knees
to scrub this beach to the bone.

If they are unwilling,
may they stand naked facing a mirror
and hear behind them, forever,
the fawning and sniveling of underlings.

MARY TALLMOUNTAIN

An Accident

An accident, Exxon called it.
No apology or remorse.
After years of dread   trade-offs
inevitable corporate masters
drove in the ugly pipeline
slicing   blazing a scar across
the underbelly of Alaska.
First strike   in the strange war
against Mother Earth

News broke, inexorably.
Black oil spill on Prince William Sound.
Exxon shrugged its shoulders,
continued operations. Soon
tenders were at work loading oil.
LATEST INSULT IN A PARADE
     calculated seizure of meager
wilderness heritage remaining
in the United States and killing
her resident creatures.

Envision: shawls of muck
     shrouding majestic old forests
     unreckoned miles; how many foxes
     other ground creatures died
     in slow drowning?

          Imagine: myriad shore birds,
               ducks, gulls, loons,

tides overtook and buried them.

Recall: struggles of otters
foundering inexorably
startled eyes imploring.

Be warned: The ancients tell us
Mother will not abide these
many "Accidents." Look to
the Ring of Fire!

JOYCE THOMPSON

Alki Beach

April 12, 1989

Alki, a civic beach. Seattle's first settlers landed here. It was November. They saw the rain, felt the bone-chill, and must have regretted the adventure. At first the settlement was called New York Alki. Alki in native talk means "by and by." Eventually our pioneers stopped looking east and named their town Seattle after the chief of the tribe they displaced. Now a seawall girds the promenade; there is a bike lane and a scenic drive. The east side of the street is beaded with eateries, apartments, modest storefronts. Seaside, the bathhouse has become an art studio, there are picnic tables and a four-foot tall replica, otherwise exact, of the Statue of Liberty, donated by boy scouts early in the century. Where the seawall ends, there is a quarter-mile stretch of sandy beach. Around the point, across the water, the city skyline rises, close and big enough to stir excitement, distant enough to be mysterious.

On summer nights, a custom of lust, old as rock 'n' roll, brings carloads of the almost and recently adult to Alki to engage in the circular, internally combusted mating dance called cruising. One usually wet and always cold night in December, families huddle on the shore around a giant bonfire to listen to the carolers on the Christmas ship. No matter what the weather, there are lovers and runners, a bold few wading, thinkers who sit and watch the tide. Tonight, a pastel mid-spring evening, anger fills the beach, four thousand strong.

Four thousand angry people, their tennis shoes filling up with sand, face a pickup truck with a PA system juryrigged on top of the cab. From the hood of the pickup, two middle-aged disk jockeys, Charlie and Ty, stare back at the organism they've called into being. Most mornings, Charlie and Ty play top forty, chat back and forth, give away free concert tickets to the ninth caller. This morning, at 6:00, they locked themselves in the station and started to play whale music instead of Michael Jackson. All day they've talked ecology. Come to Alki tonight, they said. If you're mad at Exxon, if you feel as pissed off and ripped off and powerless as we do, come to Alki. Now it's 7 p.m. and Charlie and Ty look stunned by how many of us came.

Deep in the crowd, a child attached to each hand, I'm cheered by their bemusement, read it as proof their early morning seizure of the airwaves to protest the oil spill in Alaska truly was an unpremeditated act of conscience and not a scam to fan the ratings. There is no music tonight, no politicians, no program. If the marketing department had planned all this, it would have been better planned.

The crowd, like the station's audience, is young, nineteen to thirty, mostly, blue collar and politically virgin. They were babies when my cohort was protesting war in southeast Asia, school children when we worked for a nuclear freeze. If they've taken a stand against anything before, it was school food or the new Coke. Around us, they smoke cigarettes and suck on beers, try to pacify their babies, wait for the media event they came expecting. Charlie and Ty are nice guys, not rhetoricians.

My daughter, ten, tugs at my hand, says, "Mom, when is something going to happen?" Needed: a firebrand to ignite this damp dissent.

Up front, Charlie passes the mike to somebody who used to crew for Exxon. The ex-crewman has torn jeans, a three-day beard, an Oly in his hand. "It's fucking boring on those boats," he says. "Everybody does drugs. You stay drunk. There's nothin' else to do. Exxon don't care. The only surprise is, this didn't happen before."

Sporadic grumbling, no unified response. After a too-long pause, a young Eskimo woman takes the microphone. "I talked to my brother on the phone last night, up in Alaska. He works the cannery boats. They already told 'em, don't expect to work this summer. The fish are dying."

Behind us, to the west, the sun swandives into Puget Sound,

33

chilling the air. The water darkens. My son, five, squints out to sea. "Is that the oil, Mommy? Is it coming here?"

A kid in a motorcycle jacket takes the microphone, says, "What makes me mad is, I screw up, I do time in jail. Exxon screws up, and nothin' happens." The crowd is getting cold enough to cheer a little. My daughter says, "That's not fair."

Sunset is brief, pink and diaphanous. Up front, a woman in a bulky parka says, "I'm not much of a talker, but I just wanted to say, I got kids, and I try to teach them to clean up their own mess, you know? What I want to know is, how do I make them believe that when nobody makes Exxon clean up their shit? It's like telling your kids, well, there's rules unless you're rich."

The man beside us points seaward, at three geese flying north. "Somebody ought to tell 'em not to bother this year," he says.

From the pickup, Charlie asks us if we're going to buy Exxon products anymore. We tell him no. We tell him a second time, louder. Again. Hell no. Charlie brandishes the microphone. Does anybody else have something to say?

My son plucks at my sleeve. "Don't you want to talk, Mommy? Come on. You're a good talker."

At his urging, I look into my heart, which races at the mere thought of talking: Why are we here?

My heart says, We are angry because we need to believe in the fecundity and the mystery of the sea, as if it were our mother, always there to feed and soothe us. We are angry because here, west as it gets, our frontier lies to the north; when we are ready to test ourselves or lose ourselves, when we are ready to make our fortunes, Alaska, wild and absolute, must be there with its simple, unspoiled dangers. We are angry because we want to leave our children a clean and various world, where nurture triumphs over greed.

I tell my son I'm not going to talk, because nothing I have to say would make a difference.

Ty tells us to write our congresspersons. Charlie tells us to make sure to throw away our trash. My daughter says, "Mom, let's go home. I'm getting cold and sad."

34

Closing his fist, the man beside us crushes his beer can flat. "Jeez, is that it? I was hopin' they were gonna do something." He laughs. "Shit, what could we do, huh? Exxon makes forty zillion bucks a year. Nobody here's worth over thirty grand."

My daughter says, "If I was President, I'd make the president of Exxon go to jail."

Charlie thanks us for coming. He tells us to drive home safely.

Across the water, the Olympics fade to black. The gull that circles above our heads, crying, speaks for us all. We are easier than crude oil to disperse. Tomorrow morning, our footprints will be gone.

PATRICIA MONAGHAN

There Is No Way Back

On the radio, an old friend's voice
chokes with anger and grief.
At the Stony Island intersection
I am stuck, gridlocked in place.

Stalled in traffic uselessly
weeping I listen to the news.
The light turns yellow, red
again; a sudden cry of horns.

Salmon in the tide pool, whales
beside the boat: memories flood me.
Then traffic surges forward,
each car spuming its exhaust.

Now the announcer decries
the otters' oil-soaked coats.
I speed home along the freeway
surrounded by the names of animals.

I have fished the Sound, watching
slow fog fall on the blue shore.
—Someone passes me, too fast.
I brake as I approach the exit.

Anchored over the crabpots
I have watched the day moon rise.
A red sun sets now over
the Halsted Street bridge.

I want this to be easier. I want

to forget that oil fueled our boat.
I want to hate the vivid city
as a kind of expiation.

But I've burned trees for wood.
I have boiled crabs alive.
My trapper friends kill for luxury.
Gardeners rub their hands with Vaseline.

There is no way now to be innocent,
no way for it not to be night and
each of us unprepared to pilot
through these rocky narrows.

And there is no way back. There is no
part of the world that is not part
of the world. There is not one of us
who was not on the bridge that night.

CHIP GOODRICH

I Cut Your Hair

Yesterday, the *Exxon Valdez*
struck Bligh Reef and ruptured
crude oil into Prince William Sound
and you started your period.
Cramps are worst on your first day,
it's a major spawning-ground for herring,
I was in a bad mood already,
leave me alone.

The Easter newspaper ink
smothers the feathers of black-legged kittiwakes.
The sea otter surfaces for air
and breathes oil. From the sofa
inspecting your split ends, "Will you
trim my hair?" My impotent

rage rustles the paper.
My hands shake. The print blurs.
Now, you sit so quietly under the scissors
you might be a seabird, in shock,
covered with oil, suffering my attentions.

ALICIA HOKANSON

Last of the Tribe

Halfway up the morning beach
two silvery logs become
seal pups. Orphaned
flesh opens on the deep
liquid of their eyes. Where
have I seen such darkness?

In the Hobart Museum that portrait
of the last Tasmanian, his eyes
holding all the grief of his tribe
he the last one
and knowing it.

Eye of the whale
staring out of the photograph
nearly dead gray whale, spume
of oilslick foam
crinkling around it.

In the quiet after love
and the difficult day, looking
at your eyes adrift in their
curves of skin, ocean swells
soft in a full sea, circling
the gold-brown center, I know
we must marry our own darkness.

KARL FLACCUS

The Captain's Dream

We labor over a moose calf
kill, wet hands implicated
in the steaming blood

as we sort the spilled out
quarter ton of guts and
lay aside what we can

on boughs hacked down, and you
straighten up from your stoop
midway through the mess

to look at me and our kill
gone bad, the pungence
of a fallen black spruce

and our shared sweat and
blood congealed into one,
but it is the weight

of what we have done;
the dismembering of a unity—
a love.

MARVIN BELL

The Big Slick

No one is empty or innocent.
The black lies on the white lying on the black
lying on the . . . No one is fit to judge
another's home town, not until
he himself has gone there and confessed.

I did it. You, and you, and you did it.
No one is fit to light the match,
no one may abstain for others.
We don't know how to say what a man needs
until it has been lost. Look:

I bring you the tarry stones, I draw
your hand through the gummy accretions of the sand,
but you don't want that. You want a way
to tell the worm from the fish
whenever you see a picture of the way it was.

Everyone is thirsty.
What have we done to make us so thirsty?
O Captain, my Captain! I see you.
I know the kind of town you come from.
I know the boot in the hull that haunts you.

JERAH CHADWICK

The Bog People

after the Swallow spill, Unalaska
the Exxon Valdez, *Prince William Sound*
Spring 1989

Skin like crumpled leather, slit
throats still gaping—from the peat
these bodies recovered, sacrifices to the hungry

gods of harvest, in the pictures
only vaguely human, shrunken
brown shrouds of themselves.

And the hands that held
and hurled them into the black
waters. Hands that placed the forked stakes.

Frightened or indifferent
farmers and priests, their ritual cart
empty. Our ancestors turning then

back to the small
business of living.
So today a nation

wrings and wipes. The beaches,
shuffling bog slurry, collapsed
bodies of what could be

birds. All of us
the sacrificed, turning
millions of wheels in our hands.

RICHARD NELSON

Oil and Ethics: Adrift on Troubled Waters

I live on the Northwest Pacific coast. Although Prince William Sound is hundreds of miles away, its oil-covered waters now seem perilously close. Sister tankers to the *Exxon Valdez* have passed here daily for twelve years, hidden just beyond the horizon. Until last week I rarely gave them a thought.

Now I realize their destructive potential. I fear them. And I wonder who is to blame for this catastrophe? Who will pay the costs? What can be learned from it? The answers are not as simple as they might seem.

The surroundings I live in are much like those near Cordova and the other Prince William Sound communities: forested mountains rising sheer above islands and bays; violent Pacific storms shrouding the coast in clouds and rain; the land and waters filled with a staggering abundance of life.

At this time of year, herring mass to spawn along the shores and fingerling salmon pour out from rivers and hatchery pens. Drawn by the abundant feed are humpback whales, sea lions, harbor seals, killer whales, porpoises, and countless thousands of sea birds—gulls, ducks, cormorants, kittiwakes, auklets, murres, murrelets, grebes, loons and bald eagles. There are few places on Earth where nature remains so pristine and exuberant.

This was true of Prince William Sound until last week. We can only hope it will someday be true again. Like other Americans, my neighbors and I have watched the tragedy unfold on nightly newscasts: the oil slick covering thirty square miles, a hundred, two hundred, five hundred, then a thousand square miles; sludge pluming into the open Pacific, heading toward Kenai Fjords National Park, Kodiak Island, and the rich waters of Cook Inlet.

Most of us who live along this coast are fishermen of one sort or another—commercial, sport or subsistence. What corn and wheat are to Midwestern farmers, salmon and halibut are to people here. Now, with brutal suddenness, the residents of Prince William Sound face the equivalent of a year in farm country without a drop of rain; and worse, the possibility that many more will follow.

In a state often deeply divided over environmental issues, an uncommon unity of opinion has emerged. Alaskan editorial pages and radio talk shows are filled with grief and indignation. Blame is assigned first to an arrogant and unprepared oil industry, then to an ineffective and unresponsive government, and then to a more tangible scapegoat—the captain who tested legally drunk after his tanker struck Bligh Reef.

Amid the turmoil and chaos, the anger and recriminations, it is easy to forget the raw tragedy behind it all. In 1969, I was living in Santa Barbara, California, when the first great American oil spill came ashore. Like thousands of others, I walked the blackened beaches and clambered across lathered rocks, an act not only of curiosity but also of conscience, as if simply being there and showing concern might help.

And then I found a bird, hiding among kelp and boulders just above the tide. A western grebe, big as a mallard, long-necked, with a slender needle beak, half-submerged in a puddle of mixed oil and water.

I have forgotten how many barrels of oil went into the Santa Barbara Channel, how much it cost to clean up the spill, how those who suffered damages were compensated, how blame was decided, how punishment was administered, how many animals were calculated to have died and how many were saved. But one memory is lodged forever in my mind—that dying bird, her feathers matted and shining with oil, her wings drooped, her body quivering.

She stared up at me, blinking her bright red eyes, the one part of her that still seemed fully alive. Caught in the bird's unwavering gaze, I could not escape my own feelings of guilt.

Now it has happened again, and far worse this time, on a wilderness coast populated with incalculable numbers of fish, sea birds, mammals and a diverse array of other marine life.

Each day I am haunted by images of birds setting their wings to land in the morass of crude. And I think of the sea otters, those clever and energetic creatures who add such brightness to my days, crawling out to drape themselves on oil-soaked rocks and await a slow death. Prince William Sound has become a dying grounds, filled with thousands of animals, each one another story like the doomed grebe I found twenty years ago.

Soon enough, arguments over who is responsible will shift from the courts of public opinion to the courts of law. By assigning blame we may find satisfaction. But will the legal process identify who is truly guilty? I think not.

Responsibility for the Prince William Sound disaster rests not just on the oil companies, not just on the government, not just on the tanker's captain. Ultimately, you and I must accept our share of the blame—as members of a society that understood the risks and judged them acceptable. A society that valued convenience and monetary gain above the security of its own environment. A society that placed nature outside the sphere of ethical concern and moral restraint. Each of us must accept a portion of the guilt, as members of a human community that has profoundly injured its surroundings. We belong to a society much like the tanker in Prince William Sound, laden with an enormous deadly cargo, making its way through treacherous waters with impaired judgment at the helm.

And who will pay for the Prince William Sound disaster? You and I. We will cover the cost to government when we pay taxes. We will cover the cost to the oil industry when we buy fuel or anything made with petroleum products. The notion that someone else will pay is an illusion.

There is yet another cost to us, this one far greater and more consequential. The natural world of Prince William Sound is not just scenery; it is a vital part of our continent's living community, a community that includes all of us, a community that supplies the air we breathe and the food we eat. Any wound to that community diminishes the environment we depend upon for every moment of our lives, takes away from its capacity to sustain us, whether we live near the disaster or far away, in small villages or huge cities. As we learn more about the connections among all things, we realize that damage to one place is damage to the environment everywhere. We are a part of what we have destroyed.

An environmental officer for the Exxon Corporation asserted that the Alaskan oil spill is "the cost of civilization." What we have lost may never be regained. As a society, we must agree that we will no longer accept this cost. In the future, we must be willing to pay every cost and make every sacrifice to assure that such disasters can never happen. Never again.

I choose those words deliberately. The enslavement and extermination of racial and ethnic groups in Europe and America is a deep stain on our collective memory. Behavior our society once condoned has now literally become unthinkable. Abraham Lincoln said, "If slavery is not wrong, then nothing is wrong." His plea for a moral conscience that embraces all peoples eventually became the law and practice of our land. We must now recognize the need for a further growth of moral conscience, to encompass the whole community of life—the environment that nurtures, uplifts our senses and sustains our existence.

Future generations will look back on our behavior toward the environment—the enslavement and extermination of species who share the world with us—and judge it unthinkable. My deepest hope is that the tragedy of Prince William Sound will help us toward a wiser, healthier, morally balanced relationship to our surroundings.

GLENDA CASSUTT

For Thea in Valdez

You write me your brother needs a kidney.
Soon you'll fly to San Francisco,
give him one of yours.
Before you can leave, a tanker gashes
its skin; oil slicks otters, birds.
Fish flounder white side up on thick tides.

Seen from the plane, Prince William Sound is
kidney shaped. Its amazing tributaries
flash silver, give fresh water, take in
spawning salmon. There is no organ,
no machine to absorb all these waters,
filter oil and leave the sound clean.
Its condition is critical.

Our kidneys offer a margin of safety.
Even when disease is well advanced
they continue to eliminate waste.
Some of us are born with only one.
Some of us have a sister who will sleep
under the surgeon's scalpel, allow her
vital organ to lift into her brother's body.

Shining tubes surround your bed, remind you
of phosphorous, the sea's light. You doze,
swim through black tides dreaming
a body of water can recover purity.
Salmon leap, twisting, their silver fins
the clipped wings of desperate angels.

JOANNE TOWNSEND

30,000 Birds, 160 Eagles

Whatever remembers us, finally, is enough.
If anything remembers, something is love.
—John Ciardi

1.
September: rain and the spirited calls
of south-flying geese. And of the others,
the dead and dying, they must go stiff, I think,
wings sorrowfully holding memory, that last push
to fly still in them.

2.
Size, strength, sharpness of sight,
swiftness of flight. What of raptors
can be left to poem making?

Make nests of your writing fingers, I tell my class.
Believe. See now, how we recover the light,
gold glints on the undersides of the eaglet wings
that sprout from your magical hands.

3.
How many words, deeds, to regain a world—
misty and open,
safe forever?

MELISSA KWASNY

The Archival Birds

Notice, how the meat
from its bones
has shrunken and lodged
like rocks
in the elbowed roots
of a tree. Notice,
the feathers dissolve
and the eyes, only sockets,
and where its wings,
still stretched,
are a relic of flight.

ALICE DERRY

While Drying Grebes after an Oil Spill

Port Angeles, December 1985

What does it mean to feel along a slick side
which hasn't been slick since it left the shell
for the lump that's the main wing joint,
and with as little awkwardness as possible,
lengthen out a wing?

A grebe's wings make over half its body.
Drawn out, wet, a wing is bone and a little skin.
It's the feathers which count,
row after ordered, patterned row,
feathers a person is reduced to drying,
drying a bird must endure.

Only so long. I could feel when the wing had
to be retracted, like needing to close your mouth
after the dentist has stretched the jaw to the limit.

The lively ones—the few who survived to be released—
got into action as soon as they felt warm air.
They snaked their long necks onto their backs
and rubbed their heads all over.
They poked their taped beaks into their body-feathers
and raised them, so the air could get
next to the skin and dry the down.

The raising and lowering of feathers—
its small miracle, present as miracles are
in ordinary birds in a girls' locker room—
directed the rhythm of our work:
first here, then here, now here.

A grebe is a water bird, yes, but of the earth-elements,
it has chosen the one most like air:
fluid, changeable, hard to hold, alive
with currents, light-dependent.
No heaviness. No restraint.

The grebe was merely preening, of course.
I talked of rhythm, and if I mooned about too much,
got that beak in a sharp staccato right in my belly.
"They weren't thinking anything," Bruce said when I asked.

Knowing he was right, their black eyes turned inward
to some seamless order I couldn't enter
or just plain scared to numbness—
even knowing that, after a few hours,
all of us drooping in the dryers' heat and drone,
their bodies' print on mine made me vulnerable.

On the narrow benches it was just the two of us,
the bird more important than feeling and less—
like all of life, a little boring.

What we've always wanted—to talk to the birds,
to finally get close enough—isn't what we thought.
It's the distance after all which preserves us—

all those beach walks, watching in the glasses
how a wing rows the air back, envying
the way birds ride the currents,
following their perfect drop to water,
that effortless match of mind and body—

all the times we longed for closeness,
never meaning to achieve it.

JUDITH BARRINGTON

Radio News

Dust on I-84 and the usual mirage
floating ahead; flatlands stretch
to the Blue Mountains, massaged here and there
in rhythmic circles by the sprinklers' touch.

The truck's wheels drum on concrete joins
lulling me, like some train that repeats
and repeats through dreams: *dedum dedum dedum*,
drowning the radio news with tedious heartbeats.

When the cry comes through the speakers
the truck swerves; I grab
the wheel, scorch on to the shoulder
and stop—listen to the cry of the grebe.

Its voice chokes out salt and wet winds
(blue sagebrush rolls away like smoke);
its voice describes feathers, flattened for the dive
(here, on sticky tarmac, I notice a dead snake).

The cry vibrates with guttural incomprehension,
keens with universal sounds of loss—
the wail of any living creature
brought to its knees, finally hopeless

in the face of irresistible force—
in the face of a world turned on itself,
every familiar place become poison:
pebble, wave, depth of the very ocean down to rockshelf.

Now only the voice can ride the waves

as in Valdez a reporter stalks the bird,
crouches with her microphone
and carries its thirty-second protest to the world.

Even after the cry is gone from this cracked desert
it will hover above the oil-blotched surface of I-84
but who will listen to memories of ocean, of fish,
of the time we will soon think of as "before"?

GARY OSBORNE

The Sound of Oil

Excerpted from journal entries—March 25–June 10, 1989

I arrived, forty days before the solstice, thankfully the summer one this time. Another thirty-eight hundred mile commute from Key West Florida, and now once again, I'm in Alaska and on a boat . . .

On March 25, within hours of the accident, my answering machine was receiving calls from Crowley Maritime. They were crewing up all the boats they could get in service to send to Valdez, and they needed help.

I had been down in Old Mexico thawing out after working the winter on the frozen waters of Cook Inlet. For that adventure I had arrived on the winter solstice of what was to be the coldest winter in Alaskan history. Wind chill factors of one hundred degrees below zero and more had been more than enough cold weather to last me a lifetime, but here it was scarcely mid-April and I was on my way back, back to a world reeling under the impact of the largest oil spill in American history.

My initial destination was Seattle where I would meet the boat that I would take up north. I went aboard as Chief Engineer on what turned out to be a massive old 1956 vintage tugboat named the *Sea Giant*. I had no more than reported aboard when we loaded some groceries and were underway. We were to first head down to San Francisco to pick up a barge loaded with equipment destined for Valdez and the cleanup effort.

It was a pleasant transit out through Puget Sound with good weather and a following sea all the way to San Francisco. A couple of days in port waiting for the barge to be loaded, and we hooked up and were on our way for the two week trip to Valdez. The *Sea Giant* had a type of diesel engine that I had never seen before, a huge direct reversible monster twenty-four feet long and ten feet high called an Enterprise, that looked to be right out of the Smithsonian. The boat itself is 116 feet long, of 294 gross tons, and generates two thousand horsepower with an engine speed of a sedate 260 RPM. A big comfortable slow moving relic, all in all an interesting boat. The galley has a diesel-fired range that looks like something out of an early mining camp and we have a cook named Jack who knows how to make it sing.

On the entire trip south, and now going north also, the ocean has been covered with small jellyfish that I believed were Portuguese man-of-war. They are so thick that they sometimes appear to be sea foam. One washed up on deck and it proved to be a type known as the by-the-wind-sailor, a smaller less toxic cousin to the man-of-war. This is the first time I have been on the Pacific Ocean in over twenty years and the wildlife we are seeing is a treat. We have been accompanied all along by legions of black-footed albatross. Their soaring flight, with its long low glides skimming the surface, is truly majestic, and something I have missed on my Atlantic and Caribbean voyages.

Also keeping us company in great numbers are the far traveling shearwaters of the short-tailed, sooty, and Buller's varieties. True vagabonds, they nest in Tasmania and Australia and summer along the Pacific coast as far north as the Aleutian Islands. Their journey has caused me to view my commute from a far different perspective.

The dall's porpoise with his black and white markings similar to the killer whale's has been riding our bow wave daily, while humpback whales have put in a couple of appearances also. The Pacific Ocean has been living up to its name and has been almost as smooth and slick as smoked glass. For awhile at least the tragic reason for this trip can almost be forgotten.

On the 12th of May we entered Prince William Sound, its remote beauty easily living up to my expectations, steep thickly forested mountains with immense glaciers and shimmering snow fields which at this time of year send many spectacular waterfalls tumbling into the sea. All the way across the sound, past the now infamous Bligh Reef, and into Valdez harbor we saw no sign of the spill. The *Exxon Valdez* had been moved to

Naked Island on the side not visible to us as we passed and the oil is now mostly southwest of our course. Soon enough I expect to see all too much of this catastrophe.

May 26. We have been anchored here in Valdez harbor for two weeks now and along with numerous other boats and barges we have spent most of our time standing by. The harbor is full of equipment doing little or nothing. From my vantage point, this operation is in dire need of a General. People working at cross-purposes and running in circles. We made one trip out to Smith Island and the U.S.S. *Juneau*, which is the mother ship for numerous landing craft that are being used in the cleanup. The *Juneau* is also used as a hotel for some of the cleanup crew. Smith Island is a fly speck on the charts, yet has been the center of the major part of the cleaning effort for a month or more. There are landing craft and small boats of every description literally running around in circles. I know of one beach that has been cleaned seven times. A beach will apparently be cleaned of oil and then with the next high tide, oil that is already buried in the gravel will float to the surface, recoat the beach and it will appear as if the cleanup never took place.

May 30. We haven't seen the sun in three or four days. The clouds seem almost to touch our mast, and at times the fog cuts our visibility down to a boat length. The cook has been catching a few sable fish, also called black cod; they are fine eating.

At eleven hundred hours we got underway for Knight Island with the derrick barge in tow. The tugs *Sea Fox* and *Sea Queen* are following along behind, each with a barge in tow also. Moving out to the front lines, finally, after seventeen days in Valdez Harbor.

May 31. Louis Bay, Knight Island. We maneuvered the barge in past several small wooded islands and through narrow passages up into the head of Louis Bay. It is a well-protected anchorage with numerous rocky beaches and forested mountains on three sides, the snow fields of the higher elevations sending sparkling cataracts tumbling down from granite precipice to rocky gorge. At first glance it still appeared untouched by man, and then I noticed the unnatural stillness. There is little movement beyond the falling water, only an occasional bird where hundreds once soared. The normal wildlife is absent.

Our first order of business was to get the barges anchored securely. The derrick barge anchored using a fourpoint spread which is a manner of mooring where an anchor is run out from each corner of the barge. This makes for a very stable platform. Next, the two barges brought in by the other tugs were made fast along either side of the derrick barge. This will now form a repair and supply base for the cleanup task forces. The massive crane on the derrick barge is capable of lifting boats of up to 350 tons aboard for repairs. The next arrival and addition to our growing community was the tug *Sea Cloud* with a fuel barge carrying over a million gallons of diesel fuel. This is growing into a complete ship repair facility, capable of most emergency repairs or engine overhauls.

The size of this operation is staggering. I was given a list of seven store ships stationed throughout the sound which can supply all of our grocery and personal needs such as shampoos, stationery, etc. There are hotel ships and hotel and hospital barges, West Coast boats, and boats from Texas and Louisiana. This operation itself cannot be sustained without its own detrimental impact on the environment. The amount of sewage and laundry phosphates alone, now being dumped into the water, must be tremendous. There must be upwards of eight thousand people now living and working in Prince William Sound.

June 1. We have been here twenty-four hours now, time enough to observe our surroundings, time enough to notice the heavy black "bathtub ring" around the entire bay, time enough to see the oil slicks drifting by and the tar balls amongst the popweed, and time enough once again to notice the stillness, the lack of movement in an area so recently renowned for its myriad forms of wildlife. Time enough also to listen to fishermen who have harvested these waters for years and who tell of the recent past, when I would have seen hundreds of bald eagles, plus ravens, and crows and sea gulls in numbers beyond counting, along with scores of sea otters, seals, and shore birds. What I have seen is six eagles, seven sea gulls, three ravens, one blue heron, and one otter. What has happened here is devastating and when multiplied by the hundreds of miles of shoreline affected, it is beyond comprehension.

June 4. Sunday, I awoke to find a large oil slick covering a good part of the bay stretching out from our boats. It doesn't look like the original spill; to me this looks as if someone pumped bilges during the night. It is inconceivable to me, but that would be my guess. We came here to be a part of the solution and within days we are part of the problem.

I saw a flock of seven sea gulls today, about double the number I've spotted since our arrival. This is the first time I can ever remember being anywhere on or near the sea that you could even think about being able to count gulls.

June 6. The operation centered on the derrick barge is coming together now, small and medium-sized boats coming and going in increasing numbers, loading and unloading supplies and equipment at all hours. We have daylight pretty much around the clock now as we approach the solstice, a couple of hours of twilight in the wee hours of the morning and then it is getting light again. Boats are being lifted onto the barge for repairs, floatplanes are flying in and out, and the helicopter pad should be operational soon. There is a water supply ship collecting water from falls coming off glaciers and distributing it to boats of the cleanup task force. Repair crews are fabricating parts and refueling boats; the activity is hectic and purposeful, a big change from our days in Valdez harbor.

June 10. I managed to liberate a skiff today and get out away from the hustle and noise of our part in this operation. I ran in along the shore of Louis Bay and circled some smaller nearby islands. In this area the black "bathtub ring" covers about ten vertical feet of the shore, thick, gooey, and reeking of oil—the intertidal zone is lifeless.

I came upon one group of six or seven seals. It seemed that half of them were oiled and very listless. I didn't attempt a close approach as I am sure they have been stressed to near, or beyond, their limits. There was no other life, no shore birds, no otters, no gulls, total silence prevailed.

JEAN-MICHEL COUSTEAU

Prince William Sound:
How Stable Is Stable?

I had visited the beach three times—just after the *Exxon Valdez* oil spill, during the massive cleanup, and after all cleanup workers had left the coasts of Prince William Sound. On each occasion, I kept my eye on a particular pool of oil. During my most recent visit in mid-September, the mucky pool was still there—unrecovered by recovery technology.

Weathered to the consistency of mud, this oil was a coagulated remnant of the nearly 260,000 barrels of oil the *Exxon Valdez* spilled into the ocean. According to the State of Alaska, roughly 77,000 barrels were presumed evaporated, 65,000 were recovered (but were an oil and water emulsion) and 114,000 barrels remained unaccounted for.

The unrecovered oil has been left to the winter and to nature. However, as a local resident so aptly summed up for me: "They say nature will take care of things. But even nature has to dispose of the oil somewhere."

After spending approximately $1.3 billion and employing as many as twelve thousand people, Exxon declared 1,089 miles of beach "environmentally stable" and stopped its active cleanup of Prince William Sound in September. The company planned to leave behind some equipment and personnel to monitor the shoreline and respond to emergencies.

But the "stability" of the beaches may change from one tide to the next.

I saw beaches still bleeding sheens of oil back into the water—oil that had soaked down several feet into gravel and still percolates to the surface. Exxon acknowledges this deep-rooted oil cannot be removed other than by wind, wave and water, the tools of time and tide.

These dynamic natural forces cannot make the oil truly

disappear. They can only transfer it to the atmosphere or to the sea, to the feathers of a bird or the eggs of a fish. And for how long and to what effect, nobody knows.

Scientists lack information about the long-term effects of oil, even in small amounts, and consequently the Valdez accident has become a vast experiment. Scientists are asking questions about all aspects of the spill. For example, how much oil do "oil-loving" bacteria actually love? How long does it take an oil-soaked otter to recover the insulating power of its fur after it has been cleaned with household detergent?

The sound has become a global laboratory for cleanup technology, I was told by Otto Harrison, general manager of Exxon's Valdez office. But I was stunned by two basics he said had not been anticipated by any of the oil companies involved in transporting oil through the Alaska Pipeline: namely that when cleaning up so much oil, you need a place to pump it; and that in deploying so much boom—the sausage-like barriers laid out on the water to block the movement of oil—you need to have a system of beepers on the booms that emit radio signals if any part of a boom becomes broken.

These very simple lessons were learned the hard way. But I doubt they have yet been incorporated into any oil spill contingency plan around the world today.

It is true that Exxon mounted a massive effort to attack oiled beaches. At the company's summation press conference, public relations officers laid out "clean" rocks on a conference table and spoke of how successful the cleanup had been. "I'll let you pick your definition of clean," Harrison told the reporters.

But the next day, the Alaska State Department of Environmental Conservation held *its* summation press conference, and its spokespersons also laid rocks on a table. These stones were covered with oil. Governor Steve Cowper explained how much of the cleanup still lies ahead. Other state officials circulated a list of "The Dirty Dozen"—beaches that remain ravaged by oil.

At the same time, hundreds of sea birds were still washing up dead on Kodiak Island and, though they showed no external

61

signs of oil contamination, death from oil ingestion was considered likely, according to the state officials with whom I spoke.

Thus the end of the cleanup became a war of rocks and interpretations. Your impressions depended on what beach you visited and with whom you spoke.

"There are no absolutes in this business," Harrison told me.

Except the likelihood of another accident, I thought.

Just two weeks after Exxon declared its main job over, a tanker owned by British Petroleum (which now holds the controlling interest in the Alyeska Pipeline Service Company that operates the Alaska Pipeline) lost all engine power in Prince William Sound. The oil-laden vessel was prevented from drifting dangerously close to the same location where the *Exxon Valdez* ran aground by newly compulsory tugs and escort ships.

It seems inconceivable that the sound could have come so close to another disaster, and we must ask the responsible parties how the ship could fail so fully so soon after leaving harbor. What of maintenance and crew and engine reliability? If there had been an accident, would British Petroleum have admitted fault as readily as Exxon? Would it as readily have taken the consequences?

My intransigent pool of oil didn't appear on Exxon's list of beaches admittedly "not OK yet" or on the State of Alaska's "Dirty Dozen." It fell between the lists, perhaps like many other corners of a vast ecosystem that escaped inventory or review, neither "stable" nor "clean."

It remains just what it is—a beach fouled by oil that should never have spilled, a lingering reminder not only of what happened, but what could happen again tomorrow, anywhere in the world, unless we seriously re-evaluate our system of transporting oil.

October 1989

CHARLES WOHLFORTH

Season of the Spill: A Reporter Reflects

*This is part of the one hundredth article Charles Wohlforth
wrote for the* Anchorage Daily News, *after covering the oil spill
for six months.*

. . . I never expected it to be harder to convince the world of
reality than of fantasy, but this summer, fantasy nearly wiped
out the truth. Reality was too remote, too inaccessible. It was on
distant, isolated beaches all across this part of Alaska. Some
people, if they were paid enough, didn't even believe in it when
they stood in it up to their ankles.

I nearly succumbed myself when I spent more than two
weeks in Valdez without getting out to the beaches. It was a city
of dreams, always socked in, living on statistics and the hopeful
sincerity of officials with reams of proof for something that
simply wasn't so.

Sometimes I wanted to join them. Surely it would be simpler
to pretend the beaches were clean than to continue pretending
to clean them.

At first, fighting that impulse was easy. A fantasy takes time
to gain momentum. At first it appears absurd.

Early one morning in late March I stood on a dock in the
Valdez small boat harbor when a line of about 150 men marched
past me in single file, each wearing a hard hat, a rain suit and a
life preserver, many carrying shovels over their shoulders like
rifles. As they passed and climbed onto a tour boat, I asked one
after another who they were and where they were going. Not one
answered. They looked straight ahead. Their eyes didn't stray.

About a week later I was there again, before first light, in my
own rain suit. I asked to go with them, and finally was allowed
on board. Workers told me the earlier secrecy was because their
cruises had had no destination—the boat of workers simply

went out and floated around, trying to look busy. But now, I was assured, they were being really productive.

A delicious breakfast was served on the way to Naked Island. Workers making $1,750 a week played dollar-ante poker and talked about investments. In the observation lounge, the *Sports Illustrated* swimsuit video flickered on a huge television. Men in thick work clothes rode through the chilly early morning darkness undisturbed by the incongruity of the naked skin, water and sand.

They had to be ready to accept the absurd at face value. At work on the beach, each sat down with an oil-absorbent rag, picked up a pebble, wiped it off, and tossed it toward the water. Some threw at a target to make the day go faster. When I walked along the bottom of the beach, they threw the rocks at me. Throwing the rock you wiped was important, they said, because if you put it down beside you, you couldn't tell it from the uncleaned oily rocks.

For the first of many times to come during the summer, I was a sole unbeliever surrounded by people who at least pretended to be convinced of something that obviously wasn't true.

Almost everyone had a reason that the work was worthwhile. Many said, "It's better than nothing," although they couldn't say why. Or they had to be out here "just in case." Or they were in training, learning to walk on slippery rocks so they would be ready to work on other slippery rocks when better equipment was available.

I kept asking the same question again and again. What good was this doing? George Cowie, a foreman for Exxon's spill contractor, Veco, finally said, "Exxon is a multibillion-dollar outfit. They haven't gotten to where they are by being ignorant or stupid. And they've got guys earning $100,000 a year working on this. So I basically trust that they know what they're doing."

I wrote my story for the next day's paper on the boat ride back to town—the swimsuits were on the television again—doing my best to describe how absurd the work was, and how the workers were being paid enough money to pretend it was real.

After the story appeared, some of the Veco workers went looking for me. A couple of them shouted obscenities at me in the streets and again in a restaurant. Reporters twice tried to substantiate a rumor that a Veco worker had come up behind me in a restaurant and hit me on either side of the head with the two halves of a hamburger. Creative, but not true. Later, another rumor circulated that a Veco worker gave as an excuse for missing work that he had hit me with the burger, been arrested, and spent the day in jail. This excuse was said to have satisfied his supervisors.

. . . At times, it felt like a war. That's how it was organized. There were sides, and at least some people on each thought you could say anything you liked as long as it helped your own. State and Exxon bureaucrats rarely met except in formal meetings, when their exchanges were rituals of criticism. Each lobbed a few grenades while the other ducked. Neither seemed to listen.

They even lived like warriors. They rarely left their offices, guarded like fortresses by uniformed officers with guns. They slept together in their own camps, ate three meals a day at their desks, worked long, long days and developed a bunker camaraderie with their co-workers. Most worked only a few weeks before rotating out—Exxon people called it a "hitch" or a "tour"—and the enemy never had a chance to get to know the people attached to the titles.

The oil spill was eulogized by environmentalists as a nuclear holocaust and celebrated by Exxon as a successful conquest. Writers used the war metaphor as if it were an express train to the truth and no other was leaving the station. In their articles, workers on the beaches became soldiers landing at Normandy or retreating from Dunkirk. I was guilty of comparing Valdez to Saigon.

But the war metaphor didn't really fit. Who was the enemy? Not the oil. It didn't fight back, it just sat there. It wasn't trying to prove a point. We were.

The oil was an embarrassment. Workers weren't soldiers

fighting it. They were more like partying teen-agers who had ruined their parents' carpet, trying hopelessly to clean it up before mom and dad got home.

The desperation of embarrassment motivates such madness, not the fury of war. What else could explain a society spending more than $1 billion—enough to build one hundred elementary schools at Anchorage prices—on a cleanup that was known from the start to be unlikely to work well, if at all, and which might do more harm than good? Besides, wars always end.

The war fought over the oil spill was between people. It was a war of language, and the spoils of victory were getting to call the disaster by a name of your choosing.

Each side won a few battles. Exxon turned "quitting" into "demobilization," then "transition." It changed the summer's goal from "cleaning" and "restoration" to "treatment for the purpose of environmental stabilization," forcing government agencies to retreat from "removal of gross contamination" and "removal of mobile oil."

A battle was fought over the forms used to "sign off" beaches after the goal was achieved, but since the goal was undefined, the term "sign off" could have any number of meanings. Some beaches were signed off without ever having been hit by oil. Some beaches were oiled but never got into the filing system. Others were signed off even though the Coast Guard admitted they still had gross contamination and mobile oil, because the Coast Guard wanted to fill out the forms.

It was a victory for Exxon, which used the sign-offs as miles of beach "done," and was able to claim "the last mile" on the day of its self-imposed deadline to quit, or "transition."

Almost everything got a pretty name from Exxon or the state and federal governments. Exxon's beach-cleaning chemical, Corexit, was allowed by calling its use a "test," even though the work would not involve any testing. Killing seals to study them was "collection." Animals killed by oil were called "specimens," and boats that collected them a "wildlife rescue fleet." Broken down skimmers that were anchored in place were

66

"deployed." Emulsified oil was "chocolate mousse." Floating blobs of it were called "tar balls" or "patties" in polite society, "turds" by workers in the field.

Leaving oil in the environment, to weather and dilute, to bleed out of beaches and poison seashore life, was called, "letting nature clean it up." If you can't buy a happy ending, call the tragic ending by another name.

"Letting nature clean it up" was an especially ironic phrase in Kodiak. While Prince William Sound cleaned itself, Kodiak, downstream in the prevailing currents, got dirtier all summer. Beaches were being freshly hit by oil as Exxon was pulling out in September.

Standing on the beaches of Kodiak and the Alaska Peninsula, I felt like I was standing at the edge of the world. The Shelikof Strait's unreliable horizon was a soft, smudged pencil line, losing itself in equally gray sky like an erasure at the edge of a map. Oil blobs were at my feet. Nature "cleans" itself by spreading the oil ever farther. That kind of "clean" is complete when every beach is equally dirty.

. . . Maybe the fantasy will win. Why else do people feel different now, with so little changed from the time they were outraged?

We knew this spring there was no good way to clean the oil spill. Society decided there would be a massive cleanup anyway. Coast Guard Vice Admiral Clyde Robbins, the federal on-scene coordinator, acknowledges that the political pressure for a cleanup was irresistible, and probably would have been even if science had known for sure that it would be harmful.

Decisions like this one aren't made on the basis of science. The cleanup was bought and paid for because people wanted it the way they insist on a happy ending at the movies. Why not walk out of the theater with a smile, as the director intended?

Maybe I'm just a sourpuss.

I wasn't hurt financially by the spill. Most of those who were got at least something from Exxon to make up for it. Before the spill I had been boating with my family in the Sound, but I had never lived there. I felt bad about the birds and animals that died, but they weren't pets. Their species were mostly not endangered and their numbers will probably recover.

Still, the wrong I feel has grown only deeper. Before this accident, I knew that our species was destructive, but I thought we could contain our destructiveness. I thought we could live in cities and, if our resources were gathered responsibly, there could still be parts of the world where the wilderness was unburdened by our mark.

When I helped catch birds in Herring Bay, on Knight Island, a week after the spill, I still held those beliefs. I watched flakes of gently falling snow float unmelting on top of the black oil our boat was slicing. I scrambled over an oily rock islet with a dip net to chase a half-dead duck. I felt so foolish I couldn't stop smiling.

Then, recently, I returned to Herring Bay. There was far less oil, but it affected me more deeply. I ate dinner in the rain on an oily beach. The sun was setting and a waterfall roared nearby. Although there were other boats in the bay, we were by ourselves, surrounded in one of the bay's many folds by monoliths of rock. The rain stopped. Above the mountains, the clouds still caught the light. They looked like a crocheted bedspread between me and the sky's blue, which graduated from translucence in the west to blue straight above that made me swallow deep. It was pricked with shooting stars.

It struck me then that this place should belong to no one. Only this moment should. But now the place and all the moments in it had been stolen by the inescapable oil. It was a human place now, a throwaway, like an industrial zone. Spending a billion dollars to find a happy ending had only made it worse.

JIM HANLEN

Inipol

Give me the ungloved hand. Work
is best now and old sea gulls
know I'll stick around all

winter. Oyster and mussel larvae,
the salmon smolt have left
the neighborhood. Fog is mistaken

for vapors. I have been approved.
Don't blame me for the blood
in the urine. I promise

the ground I will rid oil stained
rocks. I will clean the shore.
No bear will stay long

or hesitate here. Remember
the rash is temporary, a small
blister on the heart.

Inipol EAP 22 is the product used in bioremediation, the process which
encourages the growth of oil-devouring microbes. It contains bu-
toxyethanol, considered to be a toxic substance.

RALPH SALISBURY

Ocean Enough: Exxon's Alaskan Oil Spill

Drowned by black blood of creatures extinct
except in our engines and brains, a bird—
whose genes might have sung
in his species forever—reminds me I'm "Tsi-skwa,"
Yunwiya for "Bird Clan"
"Tsaragi, Tsalagi, Cherokee" names
"Yunwiya" 's become
in the mingling of genes and tongues.

No mingling of oil and water.
A cup of the former will seal
breakers' surface and calm, I'm told,
in English, ocean enough to save a ship,
but "spilled tons" translated as
"THE PRICE OF PROGRESS," won't save
generations become
phantoms before ancestors
disappeared unconceived.

Hunting our prairie-chicken extinct my
and my people's "lesser of evils," that kept
us from starving during the Great
American Depression,
a hunger stronger than anger moves me to say,
reverently, "Tsi-skwa," pronouncing it "See-squaw,"
thinking of mating, and birds
who may not ever be born
sing fossil-fuel pterodactyl
from engine, from ocean, from corpse-poisoned shore
into air, the name of my people a fledgling again,
to fly and, in time, in time,
to die, in an ear.

SUSAN SPADY

Glow in the Dark

A woman combs gel through tinted hair
sprays underarms   smooths on hose
applies the right tones of makeup
for her *pumpkin* and *nutmeg* outfit
earthy like perfume she sprays
a cloud to step into
as a deer might step
into forest mist

*

A man turns forty and throws a party
bouquets of forced narcissus
discs for his CD player   four kinds
of pasta in crinkly boxes
a chocolate mousse cake
Cash-or-credit?   *Plastic* he says
a toast to his future
bubbles flow in the stem
of his throw-away champagne glass

*

With his dinosaur tub sprinkler
a boy rinses suds from his belly
puts on dinosaur pj's
eats his dinosaur cookies
climbs into his dinosaur perma-pressed
sheets   his mother lines up the glow-
in-the-dark dinos on his toy chest
he dreams the relics of two ages

71

the one of the creatures
the other of plastic   their flesh

*

And the captain sails out of the bar
on a wave of Chivas Regal
in his wake an oil slick
the size of Massachusetts
the black drug pumping through veins
easing its sheen
over mirrored faces

JOHN WAHL

Human Error

SEATTLE—Joseph Hazelwood, the former Exxon skipper whose tanker ran aground and caused the biggest oil spill in U.S. history, was heckled aboard an airline flight by passengers who video-taped him and called him "a real jerk."
— The Associated Press

Who *are* you people, reeling in my face
as though it were a trophy fish,
something to boast about over lobster and beer?
Contempt goes down smooth, sure it does,
a sippin' whiskey from the top shelf;
I'd be honored, except that you're merely drunkards,
so bottoms up and go to hell.
Yes I murdered the otters, all of them,
spat Exxon's black semen into their eyes
then sought legal counsel,
rather than do the decent thing and die.
Traitor to your Cadillacs, your boulevard Land Cruisers;
oh please do forgive me, I'm nothing but scum!
You adopted the brat yet scream about soiled diapers,
such an unthinkable mess. Some slick salesman
ripped you off but good, knowing your weaknesses.
So leave me be, I can hate myself without help from jackals.
How do you know I never dreamt of saving celebrity whales,
masterfully maneuvering an icebreaker
while cameras roll and the world applauds?
'Course I'd have been drunk at the time,
botched the job you presume. Well maybe.
But then maybe I've salvaged ability,
good intentions and guts from the debris
of life's shipwreck-in-a-bottle;

will you grant me that possibility?
We're all heaped up in this together, you and I,
valued for fragmentary, specialized skills
that are a hot ticket, like microscopic gold.
Piled high and fattened on tabloids, TV,
while cyanide drips, drips, leaching away
the chrome-like robotic qualities that undergird the beast.
All the rest is overburden, trash,
tailings and leavings to be dealt with cheaply,
kept out of sight. There is always mitigation, you know.
Erector sets, video games, computer for every crib,
shopping malls filled with prowling youngsters
taught to have faith in eye-hand coordination
and a spider-trap mind. Yet the cavern dwells in everyone;
it's so easy to get lost, run out of rope
in the furthest passageway, crawling without a torch.
Perhaps my only peace of mind was found
while watching otters and sea birds,
a glacier breathing vigor into my exhausted face.
Or maybe those were but peripheral ornaments,
scarcely seen through the fog of self-pity
which I could not relinquish.
Does it matter, at journey's end? O Captain
my Captain, we held a hummingbird's heart
carelessly between our teeth
and crushed the Earth with a shrug.

JOHN KEEBLE

Tear Out Our Hearts

This is from the author's book about the oil spill, the working title of which is Out of the Channel, *scheduled for publication by Harper and Row on March 24, 1991.*

Some would argue that the damage left by the oil spill from the *Exxon Valdez* is moderate, particularly if the spill is compared to other recent "man-made" disasters—Bhopal, Chernobyl, or the continuing disaster at Britain's Sellafield. In Bhopal, some two thousand people are known to have died as a direct result of the release of methyl isocyanate from the Union Carbide installation. At Chernobyl, the number of deaths is put at thirty-seven, with an additional two hundred forty or so cases of acute radiation sickness, although the veracity of those figures is shrouded first by, shall we say, the guarded attitude the Russian government has toward information, and secondly by the unknown long-term effects of the radiation plume, particularly in Russia and Europe. Thousands more, it is likely, will develop cancers. The chronic destruction at Britain's Sellafield installation where untold numbers of Britons have had their lives endangered by nuclear waste from the world's largest commercial producer of plutonium is well described in Marilynne Robinson's recent book, *Mother Country: Britain, the Welfare State and Nuclear Pollution.* There, too, the British government, which operates the plant, has displayed a curious attitude toward presenting its people with the truth about radiation.

None of those disasters is quite the same as another, except that they all involve the release of toxic substances and that they all occurred under the cover of big money. In the case of Alaska's Prince William Sound, in which big money and a toxic, but naturally derived substance were also involved, no human is known to have died as a direct consequence of the oil spill itself, although numerous people, including the crew members of the *Exxon Valdez*, government representatives, specialists, and workers who were early on the scene, and residents of the villages of Ellamar and Tatitlek which are within five miles of the reef on which the *Exxon Valdez* foundered, were imperiled by the effect of fumes upon their respiratory systems. Exxon asserts that during the cleanup only two of the eleven thousand persons employed died on the job—one of those a heart attack casualty—and that the injury rate was thirty percent lower than the national average for heavy construction projects. Cindy Coe, Area Director for the Anchorage office of the Occupational Safety and Health Administration (OSHA), confirmed the one mortality, but added that as of December, Exxon did not have enough data to present a figure for the injury rate. This is the odd attitude toward information again, recurring here despite the argument Exxon would make for the "moderation" of the disaster. From the first days of the spill, the company has repeatedly offered unconfirmed, incomplete, and disputable numbers to further its own image.

Nonetheless, the final numbers, according to Coe, are likely to show that the cleanup effort was quite effective so far as provisions for worker safety were concerned. It's fair to add that the conditions under which the four-and-a-half months of work was performed were hazardous, mainly due to oil-slickened rocks, tricky weather, rough seas and water so cold that to fall into it meant almost certain death. Throughout, Exxon certainly took care of its own and of itself, and understandably so since the company had been consistently portrayed as dangerously inept. It's hard to imagine the depths to which Exxon might have fallen in the public regard had it, say, lost a boatload of workers at sea. This became one of the rubs as the fiasco unfolded: the growing alarm Exxon felt for the swing of public opinion and the lengths the company would pursue to influence that opinion, no doubt because of the effect opinion might have upon petroleum-related legislation.

The cleanup was striking in more than one way. There were

the hotel boats in the bays and coves, the leased-out Navy ships just offshore and the helicopters landing on the decks, the twelve thousand vessels in all, the eighty aircraft, the eleven thousand workers. Although none of the waters of Prince William Sound, the Kenai Peninsula, and Kodiak were ever quite as pristine as some would have us believe (just what constitutes "pristine" is, in fact, one of many good questions raised by the spill), the presence of industrial machinery (barges, cranes, incinerators, and diesel-powered pumping stations that droned on day and night) was mind-boggling to see and profoundly troubling to consider. In another time, fifty years ago, or maybe only thirty, we might have eulogized the display of machine and muscle, but that time is gone, even for Alaska. Still, it would be difficult to say that Exxon did not put forth a serious effort. It did. The company was called upon to do what it did best: organize and transport equipment, position that equipment, call up the specialists and the work force, make arrangements with a host of sub-contractors, keep track of the money . . . and yet to see it, to see the whitened, steam-cleaned beaches, pale as the whiteness of Melville's "transcendent horror," to dig beneath the surface of these beaches and find the oil still there, thick in the substrate, or to see the graffiti left in Valdez restrooms by grateful cleanup workers out on furlough—*Thanks Exxon for the spill*—it was finally more an act of conquest than one of restoration . . . another conquest of nature in the first instance, and of the imagination in the second. To my mind the question has become not so much whether or not Exxon put forth a "good faith" effort as it is in what does the company place its faith. This is another of the rubs. I suspect that ultimately Exxon puts its faith in the unstated but often demonstrated and now hopelessly reactionary willingness of the American people to put up with almost anything to keep the price of gasoline in the vicinity of a dollar a gallon.

The American "consumer," as we have allowed ourselves to be called, makes up by far the most radical force in the country— radical in the sense that our insatiable appetite for raw materials causes continuous and destructive change in the world and that we seem unable to attend to the effects of our habits. Our radicalism has become systemic, like an organism that learns to live out its time with a case of the worms. As a people we seem able to discern our condition, and then fleetingly, only when faced with calamity, or a sudden outbreak of symptoms, such as when one of the U.S. based but internationally connected corporations which most clearly articulate our radicalism, errs outrageously. Then, as the incident in Prince William Sound would seem to suggest, the nation flagellates itself, the press and broadcast news feed our frenzy with half-assimilated information, and we fasten on symbols by which to right our disturbing sense of imbalance, or should I say guilt.

In this case one symbol was Exxon, what many came to regard as an evil empire, though it is in fact us, and another was the otter, the newfound Bambi that we sought to redeem, and so to redeem ourselves. The first is a part of one of our society's controlling myths, the myth of endless resource and endless surfeit. Once a myth of hope and adventure, it has become a myth fueled by greed. The second symbol, the otter, conjured up the myth of the lost garden. From this springs our melancholy regard for Alaska as the last wilderness on American soil, and this is probably what triggered the remarkable but sometimes merely sentimental and so, quickly exhausted outpouring of concern over the spill on the part of the American public. What is most worrisome is that the two myths have enjoined to make the contradiction, and that the division in public personality they represent will continue our dangerous paralysis.

*

The otter itself is a "keystone" predator, a species rather like us in that its voracious appetite for shellfish is capable of causing great, precipitous change in a habitat. It is also, as Randall Davis, the Director of the Sea Otter Rescue Program, put it, the "most political of sea mammals." It is tangled up in the history of the fur trade, in wildlife legislation, in the sometimes wildly diverging attitudes toward it. Some fishermen, especially the crabbers, detest the otter. Aquarium keepers and tour boat operators love it for its crowd pleasing qualities. The story of the oil spill tends to become complicated in this way no matter where one looks. The otter has a couple of characteristics that became points of vulnerability when it was exposed to oil, first its tendency to stay near to some of the same shorelines that the oil was driven against, and secondly the loss of insulation capabilities it suffered when its fur was coated with oil. The most common causes of otter fatality were hypothermia and poisoning from the ingestion of oil as the animals desperately tried to groom their fouled fur. No doubt, we humans have our sensitivities of nature and habit. We need to breathe the air, to drink, and to eat. We are tied up with the otters in this way.

Some two to three thousand otters died in the oil spill, as did some one to two hundred thousand birds. The losses are understandably difficult to track with precision. It's a harsh, wild, large place. An oiled otter might disappear in the water or be eaten by an eagle. Later on, the eagle might die. In addition, there are the untold numbers of creatures in the lower reaches of what we refer to as the "food chain," which happens to be arranged in our imaginations a little bit like the Catholic hierarchy. The prevailing opinion seems to be that as populations the otters, birds, and intertidal life will recover, and that the thousand miles of damaged beaches will eventually finish "cleaning themselves." Some put the recovery time at three years. Others put it at twenty-five. The projected time depends, of course, upon the particular stretch of shoreline, the extent of the oiling, the effectiveness of Exxon's cleanup effort there, the vigor of the wave action, upon what is meant by "recovery," and upon the perspective of whoever it is that's doing the talking. It also depends upon there not being any more oil spills, neither catastrophic ones, nor a continuing series of small ones.

The nearer one comes to the oil spill the deeper grows the irony in its being seen as "moderate" in any sense of the word, and the more such a way of perceiving seems to become a self-destructive Juggernaut of the mind, like an oil company the size of a small nation, a blunt, all-powerful thing under which we throw ourselves. Within ourselves lives our own killer. What part of the imagination, I wonder, is brought into play and what part closes down when the hunting animal breaks for its prey, or what part closes down when it ceases even to hunt and merely allows its victims to pile up on the beaches? What keeps us from maintaining enough imaginative force to know how to draw a line like the one a half-Eskimo woman from Homer drew? When I asked her if she or members of her family had worked on the cleanup, she appeared startled at first, then said, "The sea is our sustenance. To work for Exxon now would be to tear our hearts out."

There are the effects of the second Alaska spill of 1989, too, the billion dollar money dump, the turmoil this caused in delicately balanced towns, the scavenger-like orbit of journalists, flimflam artists, social scientists, insurance agents and lawyers, the damage there, the demons it released, and the death not counted in statistics . . . the woman found floating in the Valdez harbor after a night of celebration on her Exxon money, the crew of the tugboat *Steadfast* lost off Cape Saint Elias on their way home from the cleanup, the drinking and violence in the villages. There are the people who lived inside the disaster, the fishing people, shopkeepers, the Natives in subsistence villages whose lives will never be the same again. I had the privilege of passing among them in a time of seven months following the oil spill, and I learned that the true story was told by them and by the animals, that it was a parable for the rest of us, that the question it presents us with is finally a spiritual one. The terms of the question rest in the substance of lives lived in intimate contact with the natural world and yet at the same time cast against the scrim of billions of dollar bills. The answer to the question weighs heavily upon the nature of human perception and conduct everywhere.

ORION KOOISTRA

Dreamscape

The author's family fished commercially for salmon in Ninilchik, Alaska, until the oil spill closed the fishery last year. Orion Kooistra is now an eighth-grader in Fairbanks.

It is a nice day, outside. Not a sunny day, but a mysterious one. The clouds roll through the place at ground level, like fog, muffling sounds, so it seems as if you are the only person in the world. I simply call it a place, because I am not sure how to describe it. It is slightly desolate, like a mountain top, and there are twisted hemlock trees making tiny houses all around, but otherwise there is nothing except tundra and sparse vegetation.

No, there is something after all. It is a white building that doesn't belong in a setting like this one. It is very white and modern looking. I walk, or maybe I just drift over to it by thinking. Time and distance have little meaning here. I drift in the door and see dozens of adults standing mesmerized by a work of art, trying to think of something wise to say about it. They are saying how it represents nature, but to me it doesn't represent nature, it doesn't represent anything. I ask one adult to explain it to me, but he ignores me, hypnotized by the painting. After a bit of wandering, I find my parents. They are also staring, but they do not ignore me.

When I ask about the painting, they try to explain, but I still do not understand, so I drift back into the rolling fog, back to the place that I was in originally. It's when I sit down that I realize how peaceful it is. Peaceful because it is so quiet, because nothing exists unless you turn and see the building which is standing and not making sense. Other than that, it is a drowsy, peaceful feeling that makes you forget things that are not important.

It is then that I realize that I am not alone. Out from a secret place that must have drifted nearer, comes a rabbit. It is a small brown rabbit, but there is something about it that seems different than other rabbits. Maybe it is because it does not seem worried by my presence and does not run away. Not even the building with all the adults and their art bothers it, and the more I sit with the rabbit, the less important the painting seems.

The rabbit starts hopping around, and with every hop, a baby rabbit appears. Then from all around, Animals start drifting out. Animals. The real representation of nature. And the more I sit with them, the farther the White Building drifts away, until it no longer exists in my mind.

ROBERT HEDIN

The Snow Country

Up on Verstovia the snow country is silent tonight.
I can see it from our window,
A white sea whose tide flattens over the darkness.
This is where the animals must go—
The old foxes, the bears too slow to catch
The fall run of salmon, even the salmon themselves—
All brought together in the snow country of Verstovia.
This must be where the ravens turn to geese,
The weasels to wolves, where the rabbits turn to owls.
I wonder if birds even nest on that floating sea,
What hunters have forgotten their trails and sunk out of sight.
I wonder if the snow country is green underneath,
If there are forests and paths
And cabins with wood-burning stoves.
Or does it move down silently gyrating forever,
Glistening with the bones of animals and trappers,
Eggs that are cold and turning to stones.
I wonder if I should turn, tap and even wake you.

MEI MEI EVANS

Taming the Bear

The first time, the bear was a hummock that in one slow, deliberate motion detached itself from the hillside and loped after her—more out of curiosity than anything else, it seemed. It followed her to her cabin, pawed desultorily once or twice against the hastily closed wooden door and lounged up and down the porch for half an hour, the deck creaking under its unaccustomed weight.

The next time the bear pursued her she felt her heart crowding her throat. She could hear the blood pulsing in her skull with the sound of wind in a corridor. She ran in terror to her home, closing the door with a cry against the bear's arrival on the front steps. She bolted the door just as the huge beast embraced it, pressing forward with his chest. And while she pushed bookcases, tables, and even the couch in front of the entrance, the bear began to scratch and gnaw upon the thick tongue and groove boards from which the door was fashioned.

First he swiped against the door pull with a massive paw, knocking it askew. Then he tore the handle off in his jaws, puncturing the hammered steel with his teeth. Using both paws, the bear raked the wood, then gnawed the roughened surface, shredding it systematically, taking his time. She stood on the other side, trembling, and did not know if she was queasy with anticipation or with fear.

The bear worked patiently and before long he had chewed a hole into which he worked first his muzzle and then his mouth. She knew what to do without thinking about it. As the bear forced his blunt head through the rough opening she closed her hand around the shaft of the hatchet that she used to split kindling, and hefted it to shoulder height. She hit the bear as hard as she could, not with the wedged blade, but with the blunted end. She hammered him almost calmly, and yet she used all of her strength. She could feel the density of his skull; it felt like cast iron. It was almost, but not quite, as though the hatchet bounced after each contact. Still, she could feel that the bone was shattering. The bear did not withdraw his head right away; it took five or six blows before the animal seemed to feel it. And then, when he did pull back, it was more as though his feelings had been hurt than that she had caused him physical pain.

The bear was a male. She was absolutely sure of that. It did not come again for a long time.

When it did return, it came as a polar bear, mythic in its size, its whiteness, its translucence. When she saw it step into her yard she thought of prehistoric hunters who called such creatures to themselves, courting and killing them—or being killed. She had no desire to die. She thought of confronting this immense creature, armed only with a slender spear. This bear was so big that it filled her yard. It could not have been real. It ambled across the grass, swaying on its shoulders and haunches as though considering what to do next. Deliberately, it raised its paw against the split-rail garden fence, and, as if in slow motion, pushed it in. This did not seem to require the least bit of effort on the bear's part. It stepped among the rows of August vegetables and began to dig up her summer's crop. It did this purposefully, but not with antagonism, and certainly not with hunger. The bear was methodical in his gestures. She felt that this had been choreographed, that she and the bear were merely acting out their assigned roles. She stepped to the edge of the porch, took several deep breaths, swung her arms back and forth and leaped into the air. She landed squarely on the animal's enormous, white-furred back; she felt its musculature between her thighs.

The muscles were like thick cables, hard but warm. She gripped them with her knees and calves, and grabbed hold of fistfuls of fur along his massive neck. The bear rose slowly onto his hind legs, cautiously, so that she would not fall off.

He seemed unsurprised, almost expectant, and as she clung to him so hard that her body burned, he began to lope and then to

85

run, streaming large and white, the property of her dreams. She felt hopeless. Tears streaked her face, chilling her cheeks in the torrents of wind that the bear visited upon her. She knew that the bear would never stop running, and she knew that she could never let go.

SAM HAMILL

Malebolge: Prince William Sound

"This world knows them as a blind people,
      greedy, invidious, and arrogant;
cleanse yourself of their foul ways."

                —Ser Brunetto Latini
to Dante,
            in the bowels of Hell's seventh circle,
and he named them: *gent' è avara, invidiosa e superba.*

And Brunetto said, "Know that I keep company
with clerics and with the literati
and with those who know grand fame,
and for each, the sin against earth is the same."

And going deeper, Virgil used Dante's belt
to summon Geryon from the depths,
to carry them on his back to the edge of Malebolge
where flatterers are immersed in excrement.

Teals. Terns. Eagle and raven. Sea otter, clam, and salmon.
The world's tallest mountains
are all under water. Porcupine, beaver, muskrat.
Brown bear and black bear and tiny brown bat.

The people of the soil—call us *human* anyway—
linger at the shore. We are only humus.
Bear and otter no longer out-swim us.
Loon, hawk, and wild goose no longer fly away.

Opening the heart's own book,
look! there's Dante in a man-made Hell,

entering Malebolge on the back of the beast he dreamed,
there are rivers of blood and misery;

There's old blind Homer
listening as tales of Odysseus wind and unfold;
there are tales of Tlingit and Haida and Kwakiutl;
the dance of Krishna, eighth avatar of Vishnu.

But nothing prepares the blood to assume
this speechlessness, profound silence of complete grief,
this vision of hell we can't escape
unfolding before our eyes.

Strangling on our own greedy, greasy lies,
the thick black blood of the ancient world
covers and clogs our lives.
What can be washed away is washed away

like history, tar balls riding out the tides.
We turn back to our own anthropomorphic needs,
our creature comforts, our poems and our famous lies,
closing the book on Homer, Dante, and Brunetti,

closing the book of the heart
on the face of god, and on her counterpart:
rock, fish, bird, plant, and beast:
on you, on me, and on the Geryon we ride: *Exxon Valdez.*

JOHN HAINES

Driving through Oregon (Dec. 1973)

New Year's Eve, and all through
the State of Oregon
we found the gas pumps dry,
the stalls shuttered, the vague
windmills of the shopping malls
stopped on the hour.

The homebound traffic thinned,
turning off by the roadside;
I lost count of abandoned cars.

This is the country we knew
before the cities came,
lighted by sun, moon, and stars,
the glare of a straying comet,
sparks from a hunting fire
flying in the prairie wind.

The long land darkens, houselights
wink green and gold,
more distant than the planets
in fields bound with invisible wire.

We will drive this road to the end,
another Sunday, another year;
past the rainy borders of Canada,
the wind-shorn taiga,
to the shore of the Great White Bear;

and stop there, stalled in a drift
by the last well

drained for a spittle of oil.

The driver sleeps, the passenger listens:
Tick . . . tick . . . from a starlit engine,
snow beginning again,
deep in a continent vacant and dark.

IRVING WARNER

Remembering John David Solf

Eshamy Lagoon, Prince William Sound, 1965

He dragged the record player from underneath the bunk.
"You talk about music. I'll play you *real* music."
In the cabin the lantern cast a single, brilliant cone of light.
When he put the record player on the table, I could see nicks and
scrape marks on its black case. He opened a small flap in back
and took out the handle.

He put the handle aside, slapped the Copenhagen box from
his pocket and stuffed a pinch in his lower lip; a long, lean hand
patted the record player with affection, then pocketed the
snoose.

"No cord. No power. Just wind it up and it works. The way
things should."

He savored his fresh pinch of snoose while inserting the
handle and winding. Each revolution was executed solemnly,
and his huge globular eyes and high forehead shone in the light.

"You've got to be careful not to overwind it."

The case opened, exposing the small turntable covered with
green felt. Solf plucked a bit of lint from it, nodded, then went
over to the massive shelf and bookcase that separated the
kitchen area of the cabin from the bunks. Reaching up, his tall
thin frame stretched to its full height, and when he turned back
into the light he cradled a thick record album.

Opening it, he removed a worn booklet of commentary, then
paged through wide, thick black records with faded red labels.
Finally, he removed one from its frail, brown jacket.

"The overture to *Tannhäuser*."

Carefully, he impaled the record on the turntable; the heavy
disk was so wide, it barely had clearance to turn. I had been

91

cradling my coffee in my hand, savoring his reverence for this rite, but couldn't resist a question.

"That's a seventy-eight?"

His hand stopped in mid-motion while reaching for the heavy, metal arm; he blinked patiently, and the eyes were concealed for a half-second.

"What in hell else would it be?"

The irritation in his voice challenged any other device or invention to encroach upon the moment.

Carefully, he completed the task of rotating the playing arm downward and placing the needle on the margin of the record. There was a pause to confirm that all was in place.

Then he sat.

"OK, now *this* is music."

A long, spear-like index finger released the brake, and the record came to speed within a half-turn.

From the tiny speaker unholy scratching sounds emanated, sending a shudder down my back. The needle wandered ruthlessly across the record, searching for any surviving groove upon what was now a featureless plain. I could not discern music, but when I looked at John David he had meshed his fingers together, cupped them around a bony kneecap and he rocked slowly on the stool.

After a decade-plus of play, the music that had been on that record now existed only in John David's memory, and the workings of the player only served as a catalyst. His eyelids were shut, for he had retreated into his own, private paradise. The graceful notes from the violins, cellos and French horn section filled the cabin in the grandest possible tones.

Outside the cabin, the majesty of the great spruce boughs joined in the music, and through the window I could see them lift and nod in the wind coming off Eshamy Lagoon.

On the beach, a tiny surf formed a delicate, luminescent margin of white foam.

Finally the needle swerved off the record, knocking repeatedly against the label. Very carefully, John David re-applied the brake and folded the arm back. He sighed, reached out and picked up a cup of tea.

"They don't write music like that anymore."

I nodded in tentative agreement, for he was my teacher.

During the preceding week, I had learned more than I had during any previous or, as it developed, any subsequent week. There was nothing that swam, grew, walked or flew around the lagoon Solf couldn't identify and explain.

I looked up from my coffee and saw that he looked coyly at me; a wicket-shaped hand hid half his face. He pointed at the player.

"Want to hear it again?"

I nodded and he rotated the arm downward, but stopped in mid-motion, pointing at the needle.

"I order these special from Germany."

Then he again placed it on the outer margin, took a breath and released the brake.

Around us, a curtain seemed to open, and a vast expanse of ocean glittered much as it did on the lagoon every evening. As we listened to the music grow stronger and clearer, a harmony of rightness seemed to swirl down through the trees, across the beach and surround the cabin, cradling it.

John David cupped his hands around his knee, leaned back and rocked in time to the music. But this time his eyes were open, and there was a half-smile. He had captured the moment and would not let go.

HELEN FROST

That Darkness Had No Taste

Child, there was a time when we could trust
the water. It held our weight and never
added any of its own. We could lie back,
crack the oysters open—we could trust
our food then, too. No one ever died from eating.

We slept on the water and it rocked us.

When it was dark below the water, it was dark above.
That darkness had no taste, no weight. We knew
when it would gently come, and slowly go.
When light stretched through the water towards us,
nothing came to hold that warmth away.

We rose to breathe, dove for food, the water held us.

Often, that large loud darkness passed,
but then was gone. How could we have known
it could be wounded, that its blood,
so different from our own, would not wash off,
would pull us down and hold us where no air is?

We were warm in our fur in any water.

(In my own voice, as given to an otter survivor.)

BRUCE BERGER

Time and the Exxon Valdez

The United States has been called a country that lives in the future tense. Its very constitution was an attempt to learn from history, to correct it, then to leave it behind. America was a second shot for Europe, a chance to flesh out the Puritan vision of a "shining city on a hill." For Americans, Eden wasn't in the past; it was ahead, and we would build it.

Today the most ardent booster would admit that the cities we have built do not shine. With the much heralded information age underway, we find the machine age still raging out of control, native cultures in shambles, landscapes ravaged. It is hard to imagine a truly future-oriented society having let this happen. Yet those who issued warnings—the Muirs and Thoreaus—were considered sour, antisocial, backward-looking, a drag on our destiny. They knew that history isn't left behind in Europe, or anyplace else. And now that our viewpoint is global, we see that human history is, in fact, a rogue category of something larger, called natural history.

It is against such a backdrop that the development of oil in Alaska plays itself out. Even as the fields on the North Slope were developed, the pipeline built, a supertanker port installed at Valdez, the backward-looking natural historians were forecasting disaster. While no one saw alcohol as the trigger, it seemed obvious that so deadly a substance as oil could not be extracted under deadly conditions unaided by human folly. Yet even before Prince William Sound is cleaned up and the damage reckoned, we are assured by the spillers that it is safe to explore for oil in the Arctic National Wildlife Refuge—as if human folly were a purely maritime phenomenon. As Auden has written, "The great vice of America is not materialism but a lack of respect for matter." Matter, in this case, includes all life forms not ourselves.

My father used to tell me how he and his friends would drive to the confluence of the Mississippi and the Ohio and place bets to see who could shoot the most ducks in a day. My father usually won, with totals in the eighties and nineties. Over the years he and his friends noticed a thinning of birds in the Mississippi Flyway. It seemed the sky did not spontaneously generate ducks, and my father came to support laws limiting the daily take to three or four birds, instead of that many score. That even ducks are finite may seem obvious now, but it was not obvious at the time, and if it were not for anonymous men who wrote and enforced laws to limit hunting, the common mallard would have gone the way of the common passenger pigeon. Those who said no to random slaughter were those for whom the future was real.

The pioneers of hunting regulations seem quaint in comparison with our doomsaying programmers, our biotechnologists, our detoxifiers, our environmental publicists, fundraisers and international conferees confronting problems that take our breath away. But to later generations, our own caretakers may be as quaint—and as necessary—as those who first realized that birds didn't just congeal from the clear blue sky.

It is for those attempting to clean up Prince William Sound, and those laboring to keep the oil industry—and our own gluttony for oil—from destroying the Arctic National Wildlife Refuge, that I would like to dedicate the following brief verse, written years before the Exxon spill and called "The Early Protectors":

I'm the posterity for whom you blazed the first laws
To ration the mallard and teal, to harbor the crane,
To stave off netters and plumers from flocks so dense
They canceled the sky. It was your gift to imagine
Future turned flesh, and as pure conjecture I'm
Proof the unthinkable forwardness of time
Finds anchor. As predictions with lungs let us bless
The whale. Spare the bristlecone. Keep condors alive.
Harbor the crane. For what? For themselves, of course.
And posterity, that figment, poised to arrive.

PHILIP BOOTH

A Slow Breaker

Washing on granite
before it turns
on itself, away

from every horizon
it fetched from,
this clear green wash,

the flashing, cold,
specific gravity of it,
calls the eye down

to what we thought to
look into, to all we
cannot see through.

WENDELL BERRY

Word and Flesh

Adapted from a commencement address given in June 1989 at the College of the Atlantic in Bar Harbor, Maine.

It is conventional at graduation exercises to congratulate the graduates. Though my good wishes for your future could not be more fervent, I think I will refrain from congratulations. This, after all, is your commencement, and a beginning is the wrong time for congratulations. What I want to attempt instead is to say something useful about the problems and the opportunities that lie ahead of your generation and mine.

Toward the end of *As You Like It,* Orlando says: "I can live no longer by thinking." He is ready to marry Rosalind. It is time for incarnation. Having thought too much, he is at one of the limits of human experience, or of human sanity. If his love does put on flesh, we know he must sooner or later arrive at the opposite limit, at which he will say, "I can live no longer without thinking." Thought—even consciousness—seems to live between these limits: the abstract and the particular, the word and the flesh.

All public movements of thought quickly produce a language that works as a code, useless to the extent that it is abstract. It is readily evident, for example, that you can't conduct a relationship with another person in terms of the rhetoric of the civil rights movement or the women's movement—as useful as those rhetorics may initially have been to personal relationships.

The same is true of the environment movement. The favorite adjective of this movement now seems to be *planetary.* This word is used, properly enough, to refer to the interdependence of places, and to the recognition, which is desirable and growing, that no place on the earth can be completely healthy until all places are.

But the word *planetary* also refers to an abstract anxiety or an abstract passion that is desperate and useless exactly to the extent that it is abstract. How, after all, can anybody—any particular body—do anything to heal a planet? Nobody can do anything to heal a planet. The suggestion that anybody could do so is preposterous. The heroes of abstraction keep galloping in on their white horses to save the planet—and they keep falling off in front of the grandstand.

What we need, obviously, is a more intelligent—which is to say, a more accurate—description of the problem. The description of a problem as planetary arouses a motivation for which, of necessity, there is no employment. The adjective *planetary* describes a problem in such a way that it cannot be solved. In fact, though we now have serious problems nearly everywhere on the planet, we have no problem that can accurately be described as planetary. And, short of the total annihilation of the human race, there is no planetary solution.

There are also no national, state, or county problems, and no national, state, or county solutions. That will-o'-the-wisp, the large-scale solution to the large-scale problem, which is so dear to governments, universities, and corporations, serves mostly to distract people from the small, private problems that they may, in fact, have the power to solve.

The problems, if we describe them accurately are all private and small. Or they are so initially.

The problems are our lives. In the "developed" countries, at least, the large problems occur because all of us are living either partly wrong or almost entirely wrong. It was not just the greed of corporate shareholders and the hubris of corporate executives that put the fate of Prince William Sound into one ship; it was also our demand that energy be cheap and plentiful.

The economies of our communities and households are wrong. The answers to the human problems of ecology are to be found in economy. And the answers to the problems of economy are to be found in culture and in character. To fail to see this is to go on dividing the world falsely between guilty producers and innocent consumers.

The planetary versions—the heroic versions—of our problems have attracted great intelligence. Our problems, as they are caused and suffered in our lives, our households, and our communities, have attracted very little intelligence.

There are some notable exceptions. A few people have learned to do a few things better. But it is discouraging to reflect that, though we have been talking about most of our problems for decades, we are still mainly talking about them. The civil rights movement has not given us better communities. The women's movement has not given us better marriages or better households. The environment movement has not changed our parasitic relationship to nature.

We have failed to produce new examples of good home and community economies, and we have nearly completed the destruction of the examples we once had. Without examples, we are left with theory and the bureaucracy and the meddling that come with theory. We change our principles, our thoughts, and our words, but these are changes made in the air. Our lives go on unchanged.

For the most part, the subcultures, the countercultures, the dissenters, and the opponents continue mindlessly—or perhaps just helplessly—to follow the pattern of the dominant society in its extravagance, its wastefulness, its dependencies, and its addictions. The old problem remains: How do you get intelligence *out* of an institution or an organization?

My small community in Kentucky has lived and dwindled for a century at least under the influence of four kinds of organizations: governments, corporations, schools, and churches—all of which are distant (either actually or in interest), centralized, and consequently abstract in their concerns.

Governments and corporations (except for employees) have no presence in our community at all, which is perhaps fortunate for us, but we nevertheless feel the indifference or the contempt of governments and corporations for communities such as ours.

We have had no school of our own for nearly thirty years. The school system takes our young people, prepares them for "the world of tomorrow," which it does not expect to take place in any rural area, and gives back expert (that is, extremely generalized) ideas.

The church is present in the town. We have two churches. But both have been used by their denominations, for almost a century, to provide training and income for student ministers, who do not stay long enough even to become disillusioned.

For a long time, then, the minds that have most influenced our town have not been *of* the town and so have not tried even to perceive, much less to honor, the good possibilities that are there. They have not wondered on what terms a good and conserving life might be lived there. In this, my community is not unique but is like almost every other neighborhood in our country and in the "developed" world.

The question that *must* be addressed, therefore, is not how to care for the planet but how to care for each of the planet's millions of human and natural neighborhoods, each of its millions of small pieces and parcels of land, each one of which is in some precious way different from all the others. Our understandable wish to preserve the planet must somehow be reduced to the scale of our competence—that is, to the wish to preserve all of its humble households and neighborhoods.

What can accomplish this reduction? I will say again, without overweening hope but with certainty nonetheless, that only love can do it. Only love can bring intelligence out of the institutions and organizations, where it aggrandizes itself, into the presence of the work that must be done.

Love is never abstract. It does not adhere to the universe or the planet or the nation or the institution or the profession but to the singular sparrows of the street, the lilies of the field, "the least of these my brethren." Love is not, by its own desire, heroic. It is heroic only when compelled to be. It exists by its willingness to be anonymous, humble, and unrewarded.

The older love becomes, the more clearly it understands its involvement in partiality, imperfection, suffering, and mortality. Even so, it longs for incarnation. It can live no longer by thinking.

And yet to put on flesh and do the flesh's work, it must think.

In his essay on Kipling, George Orwell wrote: "All left-wing parties in the highly industrialized countries are at bottom a sham, because they make it their business to fight against something which they do not really wish to destroy. They have internationalist aims, and at the same time they struggle to keep up a standard of life with which those aims are incompatible. We all live by robbing Asiatic coolies, and those of us who are 'enlightened' all maintain that those coolies ought to be set free; but our standard of living, and hence our 'enlightenment,' demands that the robbery shall continue."

This statement of Orwell's is clearly applicable to our situation now; all we need to do is change a few nouns. The religion and the environmentalism of the highly industrialized countries are at bottom a sham, because they make it their business to fight against something that they do not really wish to destroy. We all live by robbing nature, but our standard of living demands that the robbery shall continue.

We must achieve the character and acquire the skills to live much poorer than we do. We must waste less. We must do more for ourselves and each other. It is either that or continue merely to think and talk about changes that we are inviting catastrophe to make.

The great obstacle is simply this: the conviction that we cannot change because we are dependent upon what is wrong. But that is the addict's excuse, and we know that it will not do.

How dependent, in fact, are we? How dependent are our neighborhoods and communities? How might our dependences be reduced? To answer these questions will require better thoughts and better deeds than we have been capable of so far.

We must have the sense and the courage, for example, to see that the ability to transport food for hundreds or thousands of miles does not necessarily mean that we are well off. It means that the food supply is more vulnerable and more costly than a

102

local food supply would be. It means that consumers do not control or influence the healthfulness of their food supply and that they are at the mercy of the people who have the control and influence. It means that, in eating, people are using large quantities of petroleum that other people in another time are almost certain to need.

I am trying not to mislead you, or myself, about our situation. I think that we have hardly begun to realize the gravity of the mess we are in.

Our most serious problem, perhaps, is that we have become a nation of fantasists. We believe, apparently, in the infinite availability of finite resources. We persist in land-use methods that reduce the potentially infinite power of soil fertility to a finite quantity, which we then proceed to waste as if it were an infinite quantity. We have an economy that depends not upon the quality and quantity of necessary goods and services but on the behavior of a few stockbrokers. We believe that democratic freedom can be preserved by people ignorant of the history of democracy and indifferent to the responsibilities of freedom.

Our leaders have been for many years as oblivious to the realities and dangers of their time as were George III and Lord North. They believe that the difference between war and peace is still the overriding political difference—when, in fact, the difference has diminished to the point of insignificance. How would you describe the difference between modern war and modern industry—between, say, bombing and strip mining, or between chemical warfare and chemical manufacturing? The difference seems to be only that in war the victimization of humans is directly intentional and in industry it is "accepted" as a "trade-off."

Were the catastrophes of Love Canal, Bhopal, Chernobyl, and the *Exxon Valdez* episodes of war or of peace? They were, in fact, peacetime acts of aggression, intentional to the extent that the risks were known and ignored.

We are involved unremittingly in a war not against "foreign enemies" but against the world, against our freedom, and indeed

103

against our existence. Our so-called industrial accidents should be looked upon as revenges of Nature. We forget that Nature is necessarily party to all our enterprises and that she imposes conditions of her own.

Now she is plainly saying to us: "If you put the fates of whole communities or cities or regions or ecosystems at risk in single ships or factories or power plants, then I will furnish the drunk or the fool or the imbecile who will make the necessary small mistake."

And so, graduates, my advice to you is simply my hope for us all:

Beware the justice of Nature.

Understand that there can be no successful human economy apart from Nature or in defiance of Nature.

Understand that no amount of education can overcome the innate limits of human intelligence and responsibility. We are not smart enough or conscious enough or alert enough to work responsibly on a gigantic scale.

In making things always bigger and more centralized, we make them both more vulnerable in themselves and more dangerous to everything else. Learn, therefore, to prefer small-scale elegance and generosity to large-scale greed, crudity and glamour.

Make a home. Help to make a community. Be loyal to what you have made.

Put the interest of the community first.

Love your neighbors—not the neighbors you pick out, but the ones you have.

Love this miraculous world that we did not make, that is a gift to us.

As far as you are able make your lives dependent upon your local place, neighborhood, and household—which thrive by care and generosity—and independent of the industrial economy, which thrives by damage.

Find work, if you can, that does no damage. Enjoy your work. Work well.

NANCY WILLARD

Poem Made of Water

Praise to my text, Water, which taught me writing,
and praise to the five keepers of the text,
water in Ocean, water in River, water in Lake,
water in cupped hands, water in Tears. Praise
for River, who says: Travel to the source,
poling your raft of words, mindful of currents,
avoiding confusion, delighting in danger
when its spines sparkle, yet keeping
your craft upright, your sentence alive.
You have been sentenced to life.

Praise for Ocean and her generous lesson,
that a great poem changes from generation to generation,
that any reader may find his treasure there
and even the landlocked heart wants to travel.
Praise for that heart, for its tides,
for tiny pools winking in rocks
like poems which make much of small matters:
five snails, two limpets, a closely watched
minnow, his spine a zipper,
and a white stone wearing the handprints of dead coral.

Praise for Tears, which are faithful to grief
not by urns but by understatement.
Praise for thirst, for order in the eye and in the ear
and in the heart, and for water in cupped hands,
for the poem that slakes thirst
and the poem that wakes it.
Praise for Lake, which bustles with swimmers at noon.
I have been one, busy under the light,
piling rocks into castles, not seeing

my work under the ruffled water.

And later—the lake still sleepy in the last light—
the castle squats like the rough draft of a prayer,
disguised as a castle, which tells me
to peer into the dark and interpret shapes in the ooze:
the rowboat rising like a beak, the oil drum rusting,
the pop bottles fisted in weeds, every sunken
thing still, without purpose, dreamed over
till the fisherman's net brings up—
what? a bronze mask? a torso of softest marble?

Go deep. Save, sift, pack, lose, find again.
Come back as snow, rain, tears, crest and foam.
Come back to baptize, heal, drown.
Come back as Water. Come back as Poem.

Notes on Contributors

CHRISTIANNE BALK lived in Alaska for several years. Her collection of poetry, *Bindweed*, won the Walt Whitman Award from the Academy of American Poets in 1985.

JUDITH BARRINGTON's most recent collection of poetry is *History and Geography*. She is founder of the Flight of the Mind annual summer writing workshop for women.

MARVIN BELL's *New and Selected Poems* appeared in 1987. He divides his time between Iowa City, Iowa, and Port Townsend, Washington.

DENITA BENYSHEK has taught visual arts, dance, and performance art to children in Alaskan villages for five years. She works for Artists Unlimited, and teaches at the Pratt Fine Arts Center in Seattle, Washington.

BRUCE BERGER's most recent book is *The Telling Distance: Conversations with the American Desert*, winner of the 1990 Western States Book Award for Creative Nonfiction.

WENDELL BERRY lives, writes, and farms on 125 acres in Henry County, Kentucky. His many books include *The Unsettling of America, The Gift of Good Land, The Hidden Wound*, and his most recent collection of essays, *What Are People For?*

PHILIP BOOTH lives in the 140-year-old house in Castine, Maine, where his grandparents lived, and where his grandchildren represent the fifth generation. He is the author of eight volumes of poetry, most recently *Selves: New Poems*, and has received many honors and awards for his work, including the Lamont Prize, and National Endowment of the Arts and Guggenheim Fellowships.

SALLIE BOWEN (cover artist) has received numerous awards and honors for her painting. In 1986 she was selected from artists nationally to paint an Easter egg for the White House Easter Egg Roll. The egg is now in the permanent collection in the Smithsonian Institute.

GLENDA CASSUTT manages a Community Service Center for the City of Seattle. Her work has appeared in *Image, Whole Notes, Poet's Fair,Vol. II*, and the anthology *Tablets the Rain Inscribes*.

JERAH CHADWICK is a resident of the Aleutian Islands. His new chapbook is entitled *From the Cradle of the Storms*. He helped to

107

document the bird kill resulting from the Swallow spill in Unalaska/ Dutch Harbor, exactly one month before the Valdez disaster.

JEAN-MICHEL COUSTEAU directed the Cousteau Society's expedition in Alaska after the oil spill, resulting in the film "Outrage at Valdez," which aired on the Turner Broadcasting System on March 25, 1990.

PETER DAVISON is the poetry editor of *The Atlantic*, and the author of eight books of poetry, most recently *The Great Ledge*. He divides his time between metropolitan Boston and a salt marsh farm in Gloucester, Massachusetts.

ALICE DERRY was one of hundreds of volunteers who hunted for, recovered and washed, dried, and fed oil-covered sea birds after an oil spill in the Port Angeles harbor in 1985. She is the author of *Stages of Twilight*, winner of the 1986 King County (Seattle) Arts Commission Publication Prize. She teaches English and German at Peninsula College.

MEI MEI EVANS makes her home in Homer, Alaska. She is the coordinator for the Oil Reform Alliance.

KARL FLACCUS lived in Alaska for 11 years and spent summers exploring the National Arctic Wildlife Refuge and Gates of the Arctic National Park, and kayaking the Yukon, Koyukuk, and Noatak rivers.

HELEN FROST has lived and taught in Vermont, Scotland, Oregon, and California, as well as Alaska, where she lived for seven years—three years in the small village of Telida, and four in Fairbanks. Her writing has appeared in *The Malahat Review*, *The Fiddlehead*, and other magazines.

CHIP GOODRICH works as the Gardener for the County Courthouse in Corvallis, Oregon, and writes poems and essays whenever it rains.

JOHN HAINES first went to Alaska in 1947. Since 1954, he has lived in a cabin seventy miles from Fairbanks. His recent books include *The Stars, the Snow, the Fire* and *New Poems: 1980–1988*, winner of the 1990 Western States Book Award for Poetry.

SAM HAMILL's most recent book is *A Poet's Work: The Other Side of Poetry*. He has been the recipient of a Guggenheim Fellowship, a National Endowment for the Arts Fellowship, and the Japan-U.S. Fellowship. He is a contributing editor to *American Poetry Review*, and editor at Copper Canyon Press.

JIM HANLEN lives in Longview, Washington. He is the author of *17 Toutle River Haiku*.

ROBERT HEDIN is poet-in-residence at Wake Forest University. He co-edited *In the Dreamlight: Twenty-One Alaskan Writers* and *Alaska: Reflections on Land and Spirit*.

ALICIA HOKANSON's books are *Phosphorous* and *Mapping the Distance*, winner of the 1988 King County Arts Commission Publication Prize. She lives on Bainbridge Island, Washington, and teaches in Seattle at the Lakeside School.

JOHN KEEBLE has made seven trips to Alaska since April 1989, while working on *Out of the Channel*, a book of nonfiction about the oil spill, scheduled for publication on March 24, 1991. He is the author of four novels, including *Broken Ground* and *Yellowfish*. He and his family farm 250 acres in eastern Washington.

CAROLYN KIZER won the 1985 Pulitzer Prize for Poetry for her book *Yin*. She founded the magazine *Poetry Northwest* in 1955 and served as its editor for ten years. From 1966 to 1970 she served as the first Director of the Literature Program of the National Endowment for the Arts. She has been a poet-in-residence at many colleges and universities including Columbia, Stanford, and Princeton. Her most recent books are *Mermaids in the Basement: Poems for Women* and *The Nearness of You*, a companion volume of poems for and about men.

CHARLES KONIGSBERG is a former political science professor, and a longtime resident of Anchorage, Alaska. He is a retired Lt. Col./Command Pilot in the U.S. Air Force.

ORION KOOISTRA is an eighth-grader at Ryan Middle School in Fairbanks, Alaska.

MELISSA KWASNY teaches in the California Poets in the Schools program, and has developed a curriculum in environmental awareness for the Sausalito School District and Headlands Center for the Arts. Her novel, *Modern Daughters of the Native West*, is scheduled for publication in the fall of 1990.

WALTER MEGANACK, SR. is Chief of the Native village of Port Graham, Alaska, one of the communities most deeply affected by the oil spill.

W. S. MERWIN is the author of twelve books of poetry, including *Selected Poems* and *The Carrier of Ladders*, for which he received the Pulitzer Prize in 1970. He has travelled extensively, and translated works from French, Latin, Spanish, and Portuguese. He has also published three books of prose. He has received many honors and awards including the PEN Translation Prize and the Fellowship of the Academy of American Poets.

PATRICIA MONAGHAN lived in Alaska for many years, and now lives in Chicago, where she is a book reviewer for the American Library Association and a science/natural history/writing teacher in the inner city. She is the author of *The Book of Goddesses and Heroines*, and the editor of *Hunger and Dreams* and *Unlacing: Ten Irish-American Women Poets*.

RICHARD NELSON's most recent book is *The Island Within*. He is a cultural anthropologist who has spent twenty-five years, many of them in Alaska, studying the relationship between native peoples and their environment. He is the author of numerous articles and books, one of which, *Make Prayers to the Raven*, was developed into an award-winning PBS series.

GARY OSBORNE was the chief engineer on the *Sea Giant*, a 1956 vintage tugboat called into action to help with the cleanup effort.

S. RAJNUS (dedication page artist) lives in Malin, Oregon. She has received many awards for her work, including the Best of Show award at the Governor's Invitational Show in Salem, Oregon.

RALPH SALISBURY, the son of a traditional Cherokee storyteller, has published five books of poetry. A book of short stories, *One Indian and Two Chiefs*, is scheduled for publication in 1990.

PETER SEARS has taught writing at Iowa Writers' Workshop, Bard College, and Reed College. His most recent collection of poetry is *Tour: New & Selected Poems*.

SUSAN SPADY lives with her family in Portland, Oregon, where she tutors Southeast Asian students and raises an organic garden. Her poems have recently appeared in *Calapooya Collage* and *Calyx*.

WILLIAM STAFFORD's body of work includes many books, the most recent of which are *A Scripture of Leaves* and *Fin, Feather, Fur*. He has been awarded the National Book Award for Poetry, a Guggenheim award, and the Shelley Memorial Award. He served as Consultant in Poetry to the Library of Congress in 1970–1971, and as Poet Laureate of Oregon for several years.

MARY TALLMOUNTAIN was born in the Athabascan village of Nulato, Alaska, and adopted out of her culture when she was six years old. In 1980 she rejoined her Alaskan relatives and has since often travelled between her San Francisco home and Alaska. She was a featured poet on Bill Moyers's PBS series *The Power of the Word*.

JOYCE THOMPSON's most recent book is *East Is West of Here: New and Selected Short Stories*. Her fifth novel, *Bones*, will be published in 1991.

JOANNE TOWNSEND, the current Poet Laureate of Alaska, is an avid birdwatcher at Anchorage's Potter Marsh. She is a part-time instructor at the University of Alaska Anchorage, and also teaches a popular poetry-writing class at the Anchorage Senior Center.

JOHN WAHL is a former oil and gas exploration surveyor who now resides in Flagstaff, Arizona. Fifteen years of travel included stints working on the pack-ice of the Beaufort and Chukchi Seas, off Alaska's north coast.

IRVING WARNER resides in Kodiak, Alaska, where he teaches English at Kodiak College. He has received awards from the Alaska State Council on the Arts and the National Endowment for the Arts for his fiction, which will appear in the forthcoming collection *In Memory of Hawks*.

INGRID WENDT won the 1988 Oregon Institute of Literary Arts poetry award for her book *Singing the Mozart Requiem*.

RUTH WHITMAN's most recent books are *Laughing Gas: Poems New and Selected, 1963–1989* and her translations from the Yiddish, *The Fiddle Rose: Poems 1970–1972 by Abraham Sutzkever*. She is visiting professor of poetry at the Massachusetts Institute of Technology.

NANCY WILLARD's most recent book of poetry is *Water Walker*. She has written a number of highly acclaimed books for children, including *A Visit to William Blake's Inn: Poems for Innocent and Experienced Travelers*, for which she was awarded the Newbery Medal. She teaches English at Vassar College.

CHARLES WOHLFORTH is a lifelong Alaskan who works as a reporter for the *Anchorage Daily News*. His writing has appeared in *New Republic* and *National Wildlife*.

Acknowledgements
(Alphabetical by author)

"Word and Flesh" is excerpted from *What Are People For?* by Wendell Berry; published by North Point Press in 1990. Copyright © 1990 by Wendell Berry. Reprinted by permission of North Point Press.

"A Slow Breaker" is reprinted from *Relations* by Philip Booth; published by Viking Penguin in 1986. Copyright © 1980 by Philip Booth. Reprinted by permission of Viking Penguin, a division of Penguin Books USA, Inc.

"Prince William Sound: How Stable Is Stable?" by Jean-Michel Cousteau first appeared in the *Los Angeles Times*, October 15, 1989. Copyright © 1989 by the Cousteau Society. Reprinted by permission of the Los Angeles Times Syndicate.

"Ye Have Your Closes" is reprinted from *The Great Ledge* by Peter Davison; published by Alfred A. Knopf in 1989. Copyright © 1989 by Peter Davison. Reprinted by permission of the author.

"While Drying Grebes after an Oil Spill" by Alice Derry first appeared in *The Seattle Review*, Spring/Summer 1989. Reprinted by permission of the author.

"I Cut Your Hair" by Chip Goodrich first appeared in *Fireweed: Poetry of Western Oregon*, October 1989. Reprinted by permission of the author.

"Driving through Oregon (Dec. 1973)" is reprinted from *News from the Glacier: Selected Poems, 1960–1980* by John Haines; published by Wesleyan University Press in 1982. Reprinted by permission of the author.

"The Snow Country" is reprinted from *County O* by Robert Hedin; published by Copper Canyon Press in 1984. Copyright © 1984 by Robert Hedin. Reprinted by permission of the author.

"Tear Out Our Hearts" is excerpted from *Out of the Channel* by John Keeble; to be published by Harper and Row, Publishers, Inc., in March 1991. Reprinted by permission of the author.

"The Social Function of Catastrophe" by Charles Konigsberg first appeared in the *Anchorage Daily News*, May 19, 1989. Reprinted by permission of the author.

"When the Water Died" by Walter Meganack, Sr. first appeared in the *Anchorage Daily News*, August 5, 1989. Reprinted by permission of the author.

"One Story" by W. S. Merwin first appeared in *The Nation*. Reprinted by permission of the author.

"Oil and Ethics: Adrift on Troubled Waters" by Richard Nelson first appeared in the *Los Angeles Times*, April 9, 1989. Reprinted by permission of the author.

"Oil Spill" by Peter Sears first appeared in *The Atlantic*, February 1990. Reprinted by permission of the author.

"30,000 Birds, 160 Eagles" by Joanne Townsend is reprinted from *Cries from the Heart*; published by Wizard Works in 1989. Reprinted by permission of the author.

"Roll Call" by William Stafford first appeared in *Northwest Review*. Reprinted by permission of the author.

"Poem Made of Water" is reprinted from *Water Walker* by Nancy Willard; published by Alfred A. Knopf in 1989. Reprinted by permission of the author.

"Season of the Spill: A Reporter Reflects" by Charles Wohlforth first appeared, in longer form, in the *Anchorage Daily News*, October 1, 1989. Reprinted by permission of the author.

Editor's Acknowledgements

Many people have helped this project along, but I would especially like to thank Jean Anderson, Jean Graves, and Ingrid Wendt for their time, advice, and support. For all of that, and for the constancy of his love and interest, I am grateful to my husband, Chad Thompson. And for lifting me out of the anguish the work sometimes generated, I thank Chad and our children, Lloyd and Glen.